Advance Praise for *Being Stuck Sucks, So Stop It!*

Getting Stuck Sucks, So Stop It is an absolute gold mine. Eric Bailey provides a wide range and plethora of tools that can help anyone in any goal they have. As Eric says in the book, some of these tools seem "hokey" at first, but as I give many of them a try, I find myself more motivated and empowered to face the obstacles that stand in my way, to break down my barriers, to stretch myself beyond what I ever thought I could be, to become the very best me imaginable. Eric has his specialties, of course, but the tools in this book are presented in a way that will help anyone in any field of pursuit. Thank you, Eric, for creating this powerful, life-changing resource.

—Samuel Belt

Thank you for reopening my mind to the basics! I realized that, without taking care of my basic needs of mental, spiritual, and physical awareness, I was becoming overwhelmed and "stuck". After going through your book, I find myself reaching untapped potential and breathing new life into both my life and my business.

—Susan Bradshaw

Just finished reading Eric Bailey's book, *Being Stuck Sucks, So Stop It,* and it is nothing short of amazing! If you feel stuck in your life over anything, this is a must-read book to not only get unstuck, but to be propelled outside of your comfort zone and into your greatness. Thank you so much, Eric!

—Tom Bice

With over 90 Journal prompts in *Being Stuck Sucks, So Stop It,* there are ample ways for us to discover and own what we think and feel—what keeps us stuck. We get the chance to move from what we *don't* want to what we *do* want by working through his exercises. If you are ready to uncover what keeps you stuck, and are willing to move forward, I highly recommend Eric's teachings. Learning how to move out of depression or perfectionism is worth the price alone.

—Maija-Lisa Adams

Being *Stuck* SUCKS SO STOP IT!

YOUR JOURNEY TO GREATER FREEDOM, CLARITY, MOTIVATION, AND POWER BEGINS HERE!

ERIC BAILEY

Copyright © 2019 Eric Bailey

ALL RIGHTS RESERVED

No part of this book may be translated, used, or reproduced in any form or by any means, in whole or in part, electronic or mechanical, including photocopying, recording, taping, or by any information storage or retrieval system without express written permission from the author or the publisher, except for the use in brief quotations within critical articles and reviews.

office@feelwelllivewell.com
www.feelwelllivewell.com

Limits of Liability and Disclaimer of Warranty:
The authors and/or publisher shall not be liable for your misuse of this material. The contents are strictly for informational and educational purposes only.

Warning—Disclaimer:
The purpose of this book is to educate and entertain. The authors and/or publisher do not guarantee that anyone following these techniques, suggestions, tips, ideas, or strategies will become successful. The author and/or publisher shall have neither liability nor responsibility to anyone with respect to any loss or damage caused, or alleged to be caused, directly or indirectly by the information contained in this book. Further, readers should be aware that Internet websites listed in this work may have changed or disappeared between when this work was written and when it is read.

Tony Robbins name and materials used with permission
from TR Legacy, LLC and Robbins Research International, Inc.
For more information about Tony Robbins, visit http://www.tonyhrobbins.com.

Printed and bound in the United States of America
ISBN: 978-0-9987865-4-4

DEDICATION

This book is dedicated to my beautiful wife, Heather, who has made every good thing in my life possible. You are my rock, my source of comfort, my reason for getting out of bed in the morning. I love you more than words can express.

Table of Contents

Chapter 1: Stuck 1

Chapter 2: The Success Cycle 7

Chapter 3: Stay Motivated! 21

Chapter 4: Inspiration Blockers 41

Chapter 5: The Filters 83

Chapter 6: Like a Child 133

Chapter 7: Blue Screen Time 143

Chapter 8: Burn Your Britches 157

Chapter 9: Overcoming Opposition 165

Chapter 10: Three Pillars of Growth 185

Chapter 11: Completing the Journey 193

Acknowledgements 204

About the Author 205

CHAPTER 1

STUCK

Do you have goals and dreams you would like to achieve? Do you ever feel *stuck* as you pursue those goals and dreams?

Deborah lived near the ocean and enjoyed jogging on the beach each morning. She had a goal to run a marathon, so each day, she would push herself a little harder and run a little farther to build her endurance.

Then, one day, a typical morning's exercise turned into a nightmare.

She began her run just like any other day: a few minutes of stretching, followed by jogging down the stairs of her apartment complex, down the one and a half blocks to the beach, and onto the sand where she would run six miles down the coast to lifeguard tower 12, turn around, and run back.

What she didn't realize was the tide that morning had saturated patches of sand near the lifeguard tower where she ran.

While the sand appeared quite solid, the moment her feet made contact, she began to sink. She had fallen into quicksand, and the more she struggled, the deeper she sank. The more effort she exerted, the worse her situation became. She was *stuck*, and she didn't know how to get out.

How many times have you felt this way when pursuing a goal or dream? How many times have you put all you had into achieving something, only to find yourself in a rut, feeling unmotivated, or completely and utterly *stuck*?

People get *stuck* for many reasons, including:
- Not setting a goal
- No accountability
- Don't know how to proceed
- Fear
- Excuses
- Inconvenience
- No money
- Judgment
- Poor visualization
- Lack of inspiration
- Lack of motivation
- Depression
- Giving up
- Not having a mentor
- Only "interested," not committed
- Not a strong enough "why"
- Stuck in their head
- Self-doubt
- Perfectionism
- No time
- No energy
- Low self-esteem
- Lack of confidence
- Settling for less
- Limiting beliefs
- Lack of consistency
- Blame/victim mentality
- Scarcity mindset

Chapter 1: Stuck

- Poor nutrition
- Lack of people skills
- Self-sabotage
- Stress
- Lack of joy

… and the list could go on forever.

Write down the following in a notebook or journal:
1. Faith
2. Family
3. Fitness
4. Finances
5. Fulfillment

These are what I call the "5 F's of Success," which represent the five main areas of life.

Give yourself a rating between 1 and 10 in each of the five areas to represent how you feel you are doing. A 1 would mean you are nowhere close to where you would like to be, and a 10 would mean life is absolutely perfect in that area, so much so that zero improvement could be made. Write each number next to its corresponding area.

How did you do?

If you rated any area of your life as 5 or below, it could be that you have been, or currently are, feeling *stuck* to one degree or another. If this is the case, don't worry; you certainly aren't alone.

Once Deborah realized the severity of her predicament, she immediately began yelling for help. Thankfully, a lifeguard heard her pleas, assembled a team of fellow lifeguards, and came to her rescue. It took significant effort, special equipment, and several minutes to dig Deborah out of the pit she was in, but they eventually helped her get unstuck.

The intention of this book is to provide you with the tools, guidance, and motivation to get unstuck in the various areas of your life. As you read it, I invite you to keep a success journal: a notebook in which you can take notes and participate in mind-strengthening activities that will help you experience transformation in your life. Please do *not* read this book passively; you will do yourself an enormous disservice if you don't participate in the breakthrough exercises.

Some of the exercises may seem strange or hokey, and that's okay. You don't need to understand all the tools to use them and experience excellent results. I simply ask you to do the exercises with an open mind and a willingness to play full-on. You may find the answers and breakthroughs you need to change your life.

In your success journal, write what you envision your life would be like if you had perfect 10s in each of the 5 F's of Success. Use as much detail and description as you can.

How would it feel to have a life like the one you described?

Next, write your "why," meaning your purpose for achieving such a life. What would it do for you? How would living such a life feel?

Finally, make a list of all the ways you feel *stuck* or unable to reach the levels of life you described. What has kept you from reaching your highest potential?

I waited tables full-time for many years to support my family. I was good at it and made decent money, but I always dreamed of something more. I was tired of having to do the same thing every day, report to other people, and deal with customer complaints. Quite plainly, I was desperate for something different, but I continued at my job for several years because I was afraid of the change that starting a business would bring. I was *stuck*. Can you relate?

It took an incredible amount of faith to quit my job and start my business. I didn't know how things would work out. I didn't have a steady income from the services I offered, nor did I have a substantial amount of savings we could live on. I simply had a *desire to succeed*. It was this *desire* that helped me finally take the leap and create my company, Feel Well, Live Well. This *desire* helped me get through all the trials and challenges that life has thrown at me. This *desire* helped me become a millionaire, release more than seventy pounds of body fat, create a red-hot marriage and a magical relationship with our children, overcome debilitating addictive behaviors, and achieve the success I now enjoy.

The tools you will learn in this book work for every area of life, regardless of how old or young you are, where you live, or what your current circumstances may be. If you are ready to finally overcome your barriers, get unstuck, and create the life you have always desired, put your learning cap on, place your hand over your heart and declare, "I am amazing!"

Being Stuck Sucks, So Stop It!

CHAPTER 2
THE SUCCESS CYCLE

Have you ever noticed that there tend to be patterns within human behavior, especially when it comes to progress and success? Have you noticed that nearly all personal development books say the same things? Does that mean the journey to success is going to be identical for everyone? No, but a number of patterns will show up along the way. The better you recognize these patterns, the better prepared you will be to go through them. Oliver DeMille, author of *The Student Whisperer,* calls this "The path to all success," and this chapter is based on his works.

Success comes in cycles that contain 9 phases:
1) The Call
2) The Honeymoon Phase
3) Opposition
4) The Chasm
5) Hard Work
6) Endurance
7) Ultimate Test
8) Reward
9) Call to Higher Level

Recognizing and understanding each phase as it shows up in your life can help you get unstuck.

Have you ever felt like you were destined for more in life? Maybe at first, you didn't quite know what that meant, until one day, you came across something that tugged on your heartstrings. Perhaps someone took you to the theater and, as you sat through the performance, something in the back of your mind said, "That could be me!", and from that moment on you dreamed of being an actor. Maybe you visited a relative in the hospital, saw how well the doctors took care of their patients and saved lives, so you decided to become a doctor.

For me, it was public speaking.

I'll never forget going to my first major seminar. I watched the presenter on stage cause massive transformation in people with the message he shared and the principles he taught… and a voice in the back of my mind whispered, "Eric, that could be you."

I remember thinking, "Really? Me? Teach classes and influence the lives of others for good?"

Phase one of the success cycle is simply called *the call*. This is when you feel inspired to do something or become something greater. Perhaps you attend a seminar put on by a millionaire who inspires you to become a millionaire yourself so you can help more people. Or you might go to a health workshop and feel inspired to release weight and get fit (You don't want to "lose" weight; the subconscious mind automatically tries to find that which is "lost." When you "release" weight, it lets the subconscious mind know you want it gone forever).

Whatever form the call comes in, the most important thing to do is to *answer* the call. This means *taking immediate action* to begin living up to whatever you feel inspired to do.

I tell people who come to my three-day transformational seminars that they may feel a call come to them during the event. I ask them, "Will you answer it, or will you take a chicken exit and ignore the call because of fear?"

Chapter 2: The Success Cycle

A lot of people do the latter. A lot of people feel, deep down, they have more to contribute to society, but they fail to act because it requires them to step out of their comfort zone.

Can I tell you a secret?

If you fail to act enough times, the call is going to be passed to someone else who *will* act.

Have you noticed that, if you ignore a prompting to act long enough, it usually goes away? This is because the call was passed to someone who would be a better steward over it. What's interesting is a lot of people will receive a call, sometimes pretty strongly, but they ignore it because it isn't "logical." They say things like, "I need to think about that…" Eventually, the impression goes away because they didn't take action, and since they no longer feel the need to act, they say things like, "Oh, I guess it wasn't meant to be." Then they wonder why their life remains stagnant.

Another unfortunate problem is spouses who do not let their husband or wife answer their call because of their own fear and need for stability. I once spoke with a gentleman who felt a call to become a presenter and messenger, but his wife forbade him because she couldn't stand the idea of him not having a steady, salaried job.

When the call comes, you must *take immediate action*.

Can answering the call be scary? Yes, because it puts you on a path you have never been on before.

Can I share a secret with you?

To me, *not* answering the call and leading a life of mediocrity, without true fulfillment, is *much* scarier than answering the call. Don't worry; we will discuss how to overcome fear in Chapter 5.

Write the following in your success journal:

"When the call comes, I answer, and I take immediate action!"

Now place your hand over your heart and declare, "I am amazing!"

Once you take action to answer the call, you will move into phase two of the cycle: *the honeymoon*. It is normal to feel a sense of excitement and euphoria for a time after answering the call. You are finally following your purpose!

We see this trend in a lot of new network marketers. They feel a call to take advantage of a certain opportunity and join a particular company, and they feel so excited about the potential they experience a sense of bliss.

Allow yourself to be excited. You've answered the call! You took action to set yourself up for success. That's something to celebrate.

During the honeymoon, get as much momentum going as possible to help you get through phase three of the success cycle, which is *opposition*.

Eventually, the honeymoon phase wears off, the excitement dies down, and fears and doubts set in.

This happened to me after I accepted the call to be a presenter and trainer. I signed up for a high-level program that would give me the skills I needed. I felt on top of the world… and then the realization hit that I had to follow through with what I had committed to doing and create a return on the $5,000 investment I made with borrowed money.

I freaked out!

I came extremely close to backing out of my commitment and quitting before I even began.

I see this tendency in a lot of people who sign up for mentoring programs. They receive information about a particular mentoring program and feel strongly that they need to sign up. Then the doubts and fears inside their head begin to pick at them, and they get caught in stage three of the success cycle. Unfortunately, this is the phase where a lot of people get *stuck*. Once the excitement from the honeymoon phase dies, they quit, or they move on to another opportunity.

Have you ever known someone who seemed to have a new idea or a new business opportunity every month but never actually followed through for more than a week or two? They jump from honeymoon phase to honeymoon phase, never gaining momentum or completing the entire cycle, so their results never go anywhere.

The key to getting through stage three is *determination*.

You must be determined to follow through with a call, even when opposition arises. A way to make this easier is to *remove fear and doubt from your mind*.

Whenever someone signs up for one of my high-level mentoring programs, I look him or her right in the eyes and say, "Just so you know, you are going to have every fear and doubt you can think of go through your mind over the next couple of weeks. You will likely hear a voice inside your head say things like, 'You can't do this! Why in the world would you sign up for such a thing? You're so stupid!' You'll have doubts about the program you just signed up for, about your ability to create success with the program, hesitation about the mentor, and so on. When fears and doubts surface, grab a piece of paper and write them down. Get them out of your head and onto paper."

"But, Eric, won't writing the fears and doubts down just reinforce them?"

Only if you go back and read them.

If, after answering a call, a voice in your head says, "You are foolish for doing that," write it down, along with anything else that comes to mind. Then destroy the paper. Continue this process until you feel peaceful and more at ease. Then, *follow through with the call!*

Write the following in your success journal:

"No matter how tough the opposition gets, I stick with my call. I immediately remove fears and doubts from my mind by writing them down and destroying the paper. I solemnly commit to overcoming opposition and following through with my call!"

Now place your hand over your heart and declare, "I am amazing!"

Phase four of the success cycle is called *the chasm*. Your determination has helped you through the first wave of opposition, and you have finally gained momentum. You now experience growing pains and face unexpected consequences of answering the call.

I realized I was in phase four when the credit card processing firm my company was using decided it no longer wanted to do business with us. My company had grown substantially. We had created several high-ticket items, such as high-end personal mentoring packages, that sold for tens of thousands of dollars. I ran a client's credit card for $25,000, only to receive a message from our credit card company that it was not going to deposit the money into our account, was freezing the funds, and no longer wished to do any sort of business with us. This came as a complete shock, as we had never had any issues with this credit card company before. We never received any sort of warning that our company had been flagged nor that we needed to make changes. I remember freaking out because I wanted to get paid the $25,000, and here I was facing the realization that I no longer had a credit card processing company. More than 90 percent of the revenue my company generates comes from credit cards, so I was completely *stuck*. I had never dealt with such an issue before and had no idea how to proceed. I was experiencing a chasm.

When things don't go your way, you can either become *bitter*, or you can become *better*.

Thankfully, I knew people who *did* know how to proceed. When you get to phase four, it is absolutely *imperative* that you follow the counsel of a *mentor*—someone who has been where you currently are, is already where you want to be, and can teach you how to get through the struggles you are facing. With the help of a mentor, I was able to find a new credit card processing company that served our needs much better than the old company.

If you haven't hired a personal mentor, do so. Yes, they can be expensive, but *not* doing so is going to cost you much more. Without a mentor, you will remain *stuck* in phase four. Stop trying to figure everything out on your own. Save yourself time, energy, and a lot of frustration by following the counsel of an excellent mentor.

Write the following in your success journal:

"I always have a mentor."

Now place your hand over your heart and declare, "I am amazing!"

Phase five is good, old-fashioned *work*. You've got to put in the work if you want to succeed. Things aren't going to magically fall into place the moment you hire a mentor. Unfortunately, some people don't put in the work and don't actually "jump in with both feet."

My wife and I had an experience while on vacation that illustrates this principle.

We were staying at a hotel with an outdoor pool, and we decided to go for a swim. When we got to the pool, we stuck our toes in and realized the water was much colder than would have been comfortable to swim in.

We decided to try an experiment; my wife would enter the pool at the shallow end, starting by immersing one of her ankles in the water, then the other, then move a little farther so the water was up to her knees, then her waist, and so on, allowing herself a minute or two to acclimate her body to the water each step of the way.

I, on the other hand, decided to go to the deep end of the pool and jump in with both feet, completely immersing myself into the water. Just before I did, I was about to give myself a countdown from three to one, but realized the longer I hesitated at edge of the pool, the harder it would be. I decided to simply jump in before I could talk myself out of it

Was it uncomfortable? Absolutely! But can you guess who acclimated to the water faster? I did! With every body part my wife immersed in the water, she anticipated the discomfort of having to immerse the next body part, finally concluding with her head. From the moment I jumped in, I began to rapidly move my body around in anticipation of getting warmer and warmer. Because fear is the anticipation of discomfort (more on that subject in Chapter 5), jumping in with both feet eliminated the fear. Since I no longer anticipated the discomfort of the cold water but rather anticipated feeling more and more comfortable the longer I stayed in the water, the experience was much more enjoyable.

I realized just how similar this experience is to the success cycle, specifically what happens after hiring a mentor and moving into phase five.

Think of it this way: Imagine you are on vacation and are "sold" on the idea of going to the new *amazing* pool at your resort. As you arrive at the pool, you learn that a daily pool pass costs fifty dollars and is non-refundable. At first you think that's a bit too expensive, but you hear some of the stories of people who have been to the pool; you hear how amazingly refreshing the pool is and what a great experience it was for those who have been. So you decide to pay for a pool pass, and you finally go. Upon arriving at the pool, the first thing you do is dip your toe into the water to test how cold it is. You see others in the pool having a great time, and you think it can't be too cold if so many people are in it—but when you stick your toe in it, you realize the water is freezing.

"This isn't what I was expecting," you think to yourself.

Part of you feels ripped off. You return to the pool attendant and demand he refund your fifty dollars. He kindly reminds you that the pool pass is non-refundable, and that, if you simply jump into the water with both feet directly into the deep end, your experience will be much better.

You decide to try out the pool, but rather than follow the attendant's advice, you enter the pool at the shallow end, starting with your toes, then your ankles, your knees, and so on. Meanwhile, people in the deep end are encouraging you to jump in with both

Chapter 2: The Success Cycle

feet at the deep end, just as the pool attendant had advised, but you refuse because "that just isn't how you do things." You like to "take things slowly," and who are they to pretend to know your situation better than you do?

You continue to try to acclimate to the water very slowly, one body part at a time, all the while dreading immersing more of your body in the cold water because you know how uncomfortable it will be. You get as far as chest deep when you decide to turn back and leave the pool, cursing the pool attendant under your breath for "scamming you" and "being unwilling to refund even part of your money for the pool pass."

Unfortunately, many people sign up for mentoring programs and then, once they realize how cold the water is, don't even get into the pool. I know people who have paid tens of thousands of dollars for a mentoring program only to do absolutely nothing with it because they soon realize how much they need to get outside of their comfort zone to create change in their lives. They contact the mentor and say, "This isn't what I expected it to be! You scammed me!" The mentor kindly reminds them of the terms of their mentoring agreement and reassures them that, if they simply put in the work, their experience will be quite positive. Unfortunately, they still choose to believe it was a mistake to hire the mentor and do absolutely nothing with the program. What they fail to realize is the mistake wasn't signing up for the mentoring program; the mistake was doing nothing with it.

Just because they paid the mentoring tuition does *not* mean they jumped in with both feet. Had they followed through with what the mentor suggested they do, they would have created the experience and results they desired.

Some people only get partly into the pool. Some enter the pool ankle deep, some as much as knee deep, some even as much as chest deep, but fear of the discomfort of immersing their head overcomes them.

"I'm not going to go any farther into the water!" they say. They remain where they are for a time before eventually leaving the pool, declaring that the pool experience wasn't what the pool attendant made it out to be. This represents mentoring students who begin the journey to success, perhaps showing up to two or three mentoring appointments. They may complete the action steps they set for themselves for a little while, possibly seeing some results. But at some point, the temptation to stop growing, stop progressing, and go back to how they used to live their lives overwhelms them, so they drop out of the mentoring program and return to their comfort zone. Some blame the mentor for encouraging them to participate in the mentoring program in the first place because, again, the program "wasn't what they thought it would be."

Some people follow the pool attendant's counsel of jumping into the water with both feet, but the sudden shock created by the cold water makes them hop right out of the pool—and then blame the attendant for suggesting they jump in.

"I knew I should have acclimated slowly!" they announce. They curse the pool attendant for not giving them "proper advice" and for not giving them a refund.

This example represents the mentoring students who start off with a bang. Maybe, to them, "jumping in with both feet" means quitting their full-time jobs and going full force into starting the business. But the shock of no longer having a steady income is enough for them to run back to their old jobs and return to the security of their comfort zone, a.k.a., their old way of life. They blame the mentor for their negative experience rather than take responsibility for creating the results they desire.

Finally, there are those who jump into the pool with both feet, completely immerse themselves, feel the sting of the cold, and then do whatever they need to do to get warm, such as move around until their bodies acclimate. These people feel how refreshing the pool truly is. These are the people who achieve the experience they desire to achieve.

A small group of mentoring students jump into the program with both feet. They feel the sting of the major changes they are making in their lives, and then do whatever it takes by taking *massive action* over and over again until they figure out what needs to be done to achieve their desired results. These people achieve massive results and major growth in their lives.

Of course, some people may take longer than others to acclimate to the pool after jumping in. But if they stay in the water long enough, they will adjust, and their comfort zone—and thus their results—will grow. This is why you must never compare your results with the results of others.

If you are currently in some sort of mentoring program, ask yourself which type of student you have been. Did you sign up for a program but do nothing with it? Have you done some of the work but never truly immersed yourself in the program? Have you jumped in with both feet only to jump right back out because it was outside your comfort zone? Or have you plunged in with both feet and stuck with it, taking massive action and doing whatever it takes to create the experience and the results you desire?

Take a moment right now to write down your feelings on this subject in your success journal. If you have been doing anything but figuratively jumping in with both feet, create a plan of action to do that now. You *must* put in the work for things to change in your life.

Keep in mind that things are only uncomfortable until they are *not*. This phase of the journey will likely not be what you expected; it will likely be much, much harder. Please stay committed.

Write the following in your success journal:

"I jump in with both feet and do whatever it takes to achieve my desired result."

Now place your hand over your heart and declare, "I am amazing!"

Phase six is *endurance*. As I mentioned, some people in the pool may acclimate to the water faster than others. Some people experience results faster than others because of the Law of Gestation, which I will discuss further in Chapter 5. You cannot compare your gestation period with someone else's. The key is continuing to move forward until your goal gestates, while staying connected to your mentors. Occasionally, some people experience a very short gestation period, so they become overly confident and unteachable. Their results grow so quickly that they think they no longer need the mentor who helped them get there. In an effort to prove themselves to themselves, they cut ties with their mentor before ties are meant to be cut.

I have seen this happen more than once.

People hire a mentor in phase four, jump in with both feet in phase five, and experience such rapid growth that they fail to continue working hard and endure phase six. They become cocky, so they cut ties long before the mentoring relationship is supposed to end. Very quickly, their results plummet back to where they were before beginning with their mentor.

This happens because hiring a mentor is, in a lot of ways, like being connected to an IV in a hospital.

Let's say you go to the hospital because you need serious medical attention. The hospital staff connects you to an IV and various other pieces of equipment. You experience miraculous progress with your healing. Your doctors told you it would take three months to heal, and in only three weeks, you heal eighty percent of the way. You figure you can finish healing on your own at home. So, against medical advice, you check yourself out of the hospital—only to find your health begin to deteriorate again. Pretty soon, you are right back where you were before you entered the hospital. What you failed to realize was that it was necessary for you to stay connected to the IV to finish the healing process. That doesn't mean staying connected to the IV *after* the healing process has been completed, but it does mean staying connected with your mentors, completing the programs you've enrolled in, and seeing the process through until completion—because you never know when you may need that IV.

And you absolutely will need it when the time comes for you to experience phase seven: *the ultimate test.*

This is when it seems the entire universe is against you, and nothing seems to go your way. You may feel hated and judged for pursuing your goal. You may feel like you have lost everything. In fact, you may literally lose everything during the ultimate test. The entire world will appear to crash down around you, and you will be pushed to your breaking point.

The ultimate test will force you to choose between quitting and enduring.

My ultimate test was the first time I literally begged my Maker to take my life because I didn't want to experience the pain any longer. I didn't think I could continue even one more day, one more hour, one more minute. I felt like the world was against me, and I had to make the choice: would I crumble, or would I keep on keeping on?

Nothing can fully prepare you for your ultimate test because yours will be unique; at least, it will seem that way. The only way to get through it is to keep in mind all the lives you are here to influence for good. This was the only thing that allowed me to keep putting one foot in front of the other, keep putting myself out there, and keep doing what I knew I was here to do. Chapter 9 consists of a transcribed recording I made during my ultimate test. I included it in this book so you can get an idea of what it might be like and how to get through it faster.

The ultimate test *always* comes *just before* the reward. The night is always darkest just before dawn. So too will the doubts, fears, and trials be strongest just before phase eight: *the reward.* This is when the pressure lets up, and your hard work and patience pay off. You finally reach the success and results you've worked for so desperately. The key to phase eight is to *receive the reward with a heart of gratitude*. Celebrate your accomplishment! You've done it!

Now a word of warning: when the pressure lets off and the reward comes, do *not* become complacent. Always have the next level in mind to avoid the *imposter syndrome*, which you'll learn about in chapter 5.

This leads us to the final phase, phase nine, which is accepting a call to move to a new level of success. This can happen without you even realizing it. Have you ever found yourself reverting back to old habits or dealing with challenges you thought you had already overcome? Does it seem like things are where they used to be when you know they aren't? If you feel like you're going through a previous phase again, it doesn't mean you're going backward. It simply means you are going through the phases again at a higher level. Celebrate when you feel this way!

Write the following in your success journal:

"When it seems I'm dealing with challenges I previously overcame, I celebrate because I know I am at a higher level!"

Now place your hand over your heart and declare, "I am amazing!"

Congratulations, my friend. You have just completed the success cycle.

You may be thinking, "Eric, this is great, but what do I do if I lack the motivation necessary to get through entire cycle? What if I never get past phases one or two?"

Everyone is motivated in different ways. In the next chapter, you will learn how to find your personal "why" and *always* be motivated, even while passing through your ultimate test.

CHAPTER 3
STAY MOTIVATED!

How different would your life be if you were motivated all the time? Zig Ziglar once said, "Some people say motivation doesn't last. Well, neither does bathing. That's why I recommend both daily."

Lack of motivation is one of the most common ways we get *stuck*.

Let's define "motivation." The most basic of definitions (Oxford English Dictionary) is "a reason or reasons for acting or behaving in a particular way."

Going slightly deeper, we find that motivation is a form of *emotional energy*.

We have four major components to our be-ings: physical, mental, spiritual, and emotional. Each component has basic necessities for *survival*, high-level forms of *nourishment*, and *rewards* it gives in return if properly nourished.

For example, our physical selves (our bodies) have the basic needs of air, water, sleep, and food for survival. Our bodies cannot survive more than a few minutes without air, a few days without water, a few more days without sleep, and a few weeks without food. These are the physical needs for survival. However, we *thrive* when we receive proper nourishment in the form of nutrient-dense foods that alkalize and replenish the body, along with exercise. The *reward* the body gives when properly taken care of is *physical energy*.

Our mental self's basic need is *rest*. As long as it can rest from time to time, it will survive. It *thrives*, however, on *challenges* and *celebration*. When our mental self is properly nourished, it rewards us with *ideas*.

Our spiritual self's basic need for survival is *something to believe in*. Without something to believe in, our spiritual self weakens and can die. It *thrives* when nourished with *faith, hope, worship services, study of spiritual texts,* and *giving selfless service* and *charity*. When we nourish our spiritual selves, we are rewarded with *peace* and *joy*.

Our emotional self's basic need is *safety*. When a person feels unsafe and threatened, all other emotions take a backseat until safety—and therefore a better chance to survive—is achieved. The emotional self is nourished by *receiving one's love languages*, which we will discuss more in detail a little later, and making *passion-driven progress*. When properly nourished, we are rewarded with *motivation*. Just as the physical body provides physical energy when properly nourished, *motivation* is a form of *emotional energy* we receive when we take care of our emotional needs.

So, how do we take care of our emotional needs?

According to Abraham Maslow's hierarchy of needs, we must begin with our physical needs for air, food, water, and sleep. A person who is drowning isn't going to focus on getting more motivation to exercise; he simply wants to get his head above water. The better people fill their basic physical needs—meaning the better they eat, the better liquid they drink, the better they sleep, and the better quality air they breathe—the better they can focus on the next level of needs. These are the emotional needs, starting with safety. After that come relationships, friendships, feelings of belonging, the meeting of the *love languages*, and *passion-driven progress*.

Author Gary Chapman teaches that each of us has a *love language*, or something that helps us feel loved.

Gifts: Some feel loved when they receive gifts. On special occasions, they enjoy unwrapping presents, receiving flowers, and so forth.

Acts of Service: For others, receiving acts of service helps them feel loved. They love coming home to a clean house: finding all the dishes clean, the lawn mowed, the car washed, and so forth. Sometimes they feel loved by giving service to other people.

Loving Touch: Some prefer loving physical touch. If they are in a relationship with someone, they like to be held and cuddled. One of the best ways for them to meet this love language is through massage.

Words of Affirmation: Those whose love language is words of affirmation thrive on praise and recognition. For them, listening to meditation tracks that contain positive affirmations goes a long way.

Quality Time: Finally, there are those whose love language is quality time with their loved ones. These are the people who prioritize spending time with family and friends in fun, uplifting situations.

With our emotional needs met, we are motivated to fill the next level of needs, our mental needs. Creating a proper balance of mental challenges, rest, relaxation, and celebration provides nourishment to come up with ideas that lead to prestige and accomplishments.

At the highest level are our spiritual needs. It is extremely important to have something to believe in. Nourishing our spiritual selves with faith, proper worship services, hope, and charity allows us to reach our highest potential, which gives us feelings of peace, joy, and fulfillment.

So, where do you begin?

Start by getting proper nutrition, breathing quality air that is free from pollution, and making sure to get enough sleep. Make it a priority to have your love languages met. Spend time on things you are passionate about. Allow time for mental stimulation, relaxation, and celebration. Increase your spiritual convictions through acts of faith, proper worship, the study of spiritual texts, and giving selfless service.

"Eric, that seems like a lot! How do I keep from feeling overwhelmed?"

Overwhelm is a common way we get *stuck*. Thankfully, overwhelm can be countered by *chunking*.

It is easy to fall into the trap of focusing on too much at once. This creates overwhelm and loss of motivation. For example, some people set out to lose one hundred pounds of body fat but soon lose motivation because they realize doing so may require years of hard work. They think, "Why bother trying?"

If they focus on simply releasing one or two pounds each week and repeating the process, it seems much more doable.

Renowned street performer David Blaine used this method to his advantage when he performed one of his incredible acts of endurance, spending sixty-three straight hours inside a block of ice. His goal was to break the world record of sixty hours, but he made it a point *not* to focus on the sixty hours as a whole. Instead, he focused on enduring one hour at a time. He repeated to himself, "I just need to get through this next hour..." Soon he had smashed the world record and proved that a feat of endurance is possible with the right mindset.

If you find yourself feeling overwhelmed, make a list of everything you need to do. Next, group similar tasks, or tasks that can be done in tandem, together. For example, if you have "buy groceries" and "shop for office supplies" on your list, you might group those tasks together if you can complete both during the same trip. Once you have grouped, or *chunked,* similar tasks, make a plan of action by scheduling when you will accomplish each chunk of tasks. Having a clear plan of action can lessen feelings of overwhelm. Whenever possible, delegating specific tasks to others can facilitate this process.

"But, Eric, I just don't think I can do it. I'm not Superman, after all!"

Chapter 3: Stay Motivated!

Motivation is strongly influenced by what we *identify with,* particularly when it comes to what we say about ourselves. Someone who identifies as a smoker will be much less motivated to avoid tobacco than someone who identifies as a nonsmoker. This is why those who desire to quit smoking (or any other addictive behavior) must *never* use the phrase, "I am an addict…"

Our *identity* plays a large role in what we are motivated to do. For example, those who label themselves as "fat," "unworthy," "stupid," "addict," "incapable," and the like tend to live up to those labels. Someone who identifies as a smoker may go a period of time without smoking, but eventually, one of two things takes place: either he will revert to smoking, or he will change his identity to that of nonsmoker. This is known as *The Pygmalion Effect,* meaning, the tendency to live up to expectations or labels given to a person, including labeling yourself, both positively and negatively. Giving yourself negative labels sabotages you, which inevitably leads to being *stuck.*

If you *must* discuss a struggle you are working to overcome, such as an addiction to alcohol, replace the phrase, "I am an alcoholic," with more empowering phrases, such as, "I am overcoming an addiction to alcohol." The first phrase reinforces the addictive behavior at an identity level, while the second separates the addictive behavior from the identity.

The words, "I am…" are extremely powerful. Only follow them with positive words.

In your success journal, make a list of positive affirmations that begin with, "I am…" Place your list on the wall and repeat out loud each morning, with your hand over your heart. This allows you to use the Pygmalion Effect in your favor; you now have positive labels you've given yourself.

The way you talk about yourself also affects your confidence, which in turn affects your results. The more confident you are that you will achieve something, the more motivated you will be to achieve it. If two people are running a marathon for the first time, the person who says, "I really *hope* I cross the finish line" will have a much harder time staying motivated and completing the task than someone who says, "I *know* I will cross the finish line!"

A number of years ago, I was invited to work out with a world body-building champion who asked me to meet him on the football field of a local high school. After I arrived, he challenged me to a race across the football field. The catch was that we wouldn't run across the field; we would do lunges across the field and back. I wasn't exactly a fitness expert at that time, let alone a world body-building champion, so it goes without saying that he was ahead of me for the majority of the competition.

I remember thinking, "I am so tired! There's no way I can go on!"

Then I remembered a technique developed by my good friend Noah St. John, called *afformations*, which are declarations in the form of a "why" question. When we ask ourselves "why" questions, our brain automatically goes to work looking for the answer.

I asked myself, "Why do I have unlimited strength and energy? Why do I have unlimited strength and energy? Why do I have unlimited strength and energy?"

My speed increased dramatically, and I ended up beating Mr. Universe to the end of the field during our final lap across.

"What just happened?", he asked me in shock. "You were going so slowly, when suddenly you got this mega burst of energy and speed. What did you do?"

I smiled as I told him about *afformations*.

If you believe you have little motivation or willpower, that's exactly what you are going to manifest. If you choose to believe you have *unlimited* willpower, *unlimited* strength, *unlimited* energy, you can accomplish anything!

Chapter 3: Stay Motivated!

Write the following in your success journal:
"Why do I have unlimited motivation?
Why do I have unlimited motivation?
Why do I have unlimited motivation?"
Now place your hand over your heart and declare, "I am amazing!"
Some additional tips when it comes to motivation include:

- Replace low-level thinking with high-level thinking. Instead of focusing on *what* you want to achieve or *how* you're going to achieve it, first focus on *why* you want to achieve it. When your *why* is great enough, the *how* will present itself.
- Surround yourself with people who motivate you. According to motivational speaker Jim Rohn, "You are the average of the five people you spend the most time with." Your *network* equals your *net worth.* Choose your friends and associates wisely. Make sure you spend most of your time with people who encourage and support you rather than people who poke fun at you, judge, gossip and discourage you, or support unproductive behavior. There is a major difference between a *friend* and an *accomplice. Friends* help you become your best self. *Accomplices* keep you *stuck.*
- Read motivational stories, books, and quotes. A few of my favorite quotes include:
  - "You can't cross the sea merely by standing and staring at the water." —Rabindranath Tagore, poet, writer and composer
  - "Only I can change my life; no one can change it for me."— Carol Burnett, comedian
  - "For things to change, I must change. For things to improve, I must improve." —Jim Rohn
  - "Don't wish things were easier. Wish that you were better." —Jim Rohn
  - "The only time success comes before work is in the dictionary." —sportswriter Stubby Currence

- ▸ "Don't limit your challenges, challenge your limits." —Jerry Dunn, college basketball coach
- ▸ "Great things never came from comfort zones." —Anonymous
- ▸ "Tough times never last, but tough people do." —Robert H. Schuller
- ▸ "Be the one percent that is willing to do what ninety-nine percent aren't." —Unknown
- ▸ "There are no mistakes, only learning experiences." —Unknown
- ▸ "I'd rather attempt to do something great and fail than attempt to do nothing and succeed." —Robert H. Schuller

If there comes a time when you feel unmotivated or *stuck*—perhaps you don't know what you want to work on or how to go about working on it—a part of you may not feel completely *fulfilled*. A lack of fulfillment, however you define it, can leave you feeling down, unmotivated, and extremely *stuck*.

Write the following list of feelings in your success journal:

- Love
- Joy
- Happiness
- Peace
- Security
- Fulfillment
- Pleasure
- Acceptance
- Respect
- Admiration

Now put these ten feelings in order of importance to you, starting whatever you feel is the most important, and ending with whatever you feel is least important.

Once you've done so, add the five love languages:

- Words of affirmation
- Quality time together
- Acts of service
- Gifts
- Loving touch

Put the love languages in your order of importance, again starting with whichever one you feel is most important and ending with the least important.

Once you've done that, I have a secret to tell you.

Are you ready for it?

I'm not a betting man, but if I were, I would guess the feeling at the top of your list (which we will refer to as your *favorite feeling*) and the love language you put at the top of your list (which we will refer to as your *primary love language*) are what you aren't receiving enough of.

FF + PLL + PDP = PFF.

In other words, your *favorite feeling* plus your *primary love language* plus *passion-driven progress* make up your *personal fulfillment formula*. For example, if your favorite feeling is joy, your primary love language is words of affirmation, and you are taking regular action to move forward with your passions, your *personal fulfillment formula* would be joy + words of affirmation + passion-driven progress, which will be discussed shortly. When you get enough of each, your *fulfillment tank* is full, and life is good. When you do not, you can feel *stuck*.

Write down the following in your success journal:
- Self
- Higher Power
- Family
- Career
- Other people

Next, rate on a scale of 1 to 10 how much you feel you receive your favorite feeling from each of the five areas, with 1 representing receiving very little of your favorite feeling, and 10 representing feeling totally and completely fulfilled by your favorite feeling.

Repeat this process with your primary love language in each of the five areas.

Passion-driven progress comes from identifying your greatest passion and taking daily action steps to progress with it. For example, if your greatest passion is cooking, you would want to include cooking as a regular part of your life in ways that create progress. You might work to perfect a particular dish, gather recipes to include in a cookbook you could then publish, take classes from master chefs to learn different cooking techniques—whatever will help you progress. *Happiness* comes from *progress*, and *happiness* helps you get *unstuck*.

In your success journal, write down your greatest passion and how much you make it part of your daily life on a scale of 1 to 10, with 1 representing almost never, and 10 representing regularly participating in your passion and feeling totally and completely fulfilled.

How did you do?

If you are feeling *stuck* or unmotivated, there's a good chance you do not feel totally fulfilled. If you gave yourself anything less than a 10 for your greatest passion, set daily *inspired action steps* to include your passion in your life on a more regular basis and make further progress. We will discuss how to receive inspired action steps in Chapter 4.

In your success journal, set specific action steps to improve any area you rated less than a perfect 10. For example, if your primary love language is loving touch, and you gave yourself a 5 in the category of other people, you might set the action step of giving at least ten heart-to-heart hugs each day. If your favorite feeling is peace, and you gave yourself a 3 in the Higher Power category, it may mean that areas of your life are not in harmony with your spiritual beliefs, so you might set action steps to eliminate behaviors and habits that are keeping you out of alignment with your Higher Power.

(If you are currently struggling with *addictive* behaviors and are ready to eliminate them once and for all, please contact me directly by sending an email to Eric@FeelWellLiveWell.com right away, with the subject "I am ready to change!". In the email, briefly explain the struggles you are facing. I may have a solution to help you eradicate the addictive behavior.)

Completing these action steps will help you feel more fulfilled, get unstuck, and increase levels of performance.

Another reason people feel *stuck* is because they lack *purpose*, meaning, their *why* for doing what they say they want to do.

In your success journal, write down a major goal you are working on but have been struggling to achieve and/or stay motivated to get. This may be a goal to release weight, start a business, or add a number of people to a network marketing downline. Whatever it is, write it down at the top of the page.

Next, create a *Want it List,* meaning a list of all the reasons you want to achieve your goal. Be as detailed as possible.

Once that is complete, rate how strongly you want to achieve your goal on a scale of 0 to 100, 0 meaning you absolutely do *not* want to achieve it, and 100 meaning you are perfectly motivated and feel absolutely unstoppable. Don't stop and think about it. Simply tap into your intuition and write down the first number between 0 and 100 that comes to your mind, even if it doesn't seem to make sense or if the number seems really low.

If you feel *stuck* and have been struggling to achieve this goal, how much you want to achieve it probably isn't as high as it needs to be for you to do what it takes.

Next, create a *Do Not Want It List,* meaning a list of all the reasons you *do not* want to achieve this goal. Include all the excuses you've made for why you haven't achieved it already. If you have a fitness goal, maybe your reasons on this list include such things as: "I don't like to exercise," or "I don't want to give up chocolate." Come on, be honest with yourself. This is not a trick question. Make a full list of all the reasons you *do not* want to achieve your goal.

Just as you did with your *Want It List*, rate how strongly you *do not* want to achieve your goal on a scale of 0 to 100, 0 meaning there is absolutely nothing on your *Do Not Want It List* and everything about the process of achieving your goal gives you immense satisfaction, and 100 being the exact opposite, meaning you believe the process of achieving your goal would give you excruciating amounts of pain. Be completely honest with yourself and intuitively write the first number from 0 to 100 that comes to your mind.

Once you do, note which number between your *Want It List* and your *Do Not Want It List* is higher.

One of reasons people fail to reach certain goals is because their *Do Not Want It List* is too strong.

"Change happens when the pain of staying the same is greater than the pain of change," says popular life coach, Tony Robbins. If your *Want It List* was 100 and your *Do Not Want It List* was 0, you would be unstoppable. Your desire to reach your goal would be so high, you wouldn't let anything get in your way. You would find the resources and the mentor you need; you would put in the time, invest the money, put forth the effort—whatever it takes. Being *stuck* would never be an issue.

So, how do you get the strength of your *Want It List* to 100 and your *Don't Want It List* to 0?

First, recognize what motivators are driving your *Want It List*.

There are four levels of motivation: *consequence, social, agent,* and *charity*.

We do things at a *consequence level* to either avoid a punishment or gain a reward. For example, many people begin the process of slimming down because their doctor tells them if they don't, they will develop diabetes or some kind of heart condition. Children often comply with household rules to avoid getting a "time out" or to receive some sort of treat.

Go through the reasons you wrote in your *Want It List* and put an X next to each reason that could be classified as a consequence-level motivator.

We do things at a *social level* because we "should" do them, or because others "expect us" to do so. Many company employees exist at this level of motivation. They complete their tasks because they are expected to do so. At times, this is mixed with the consequence-level motivators of avoiding being fired and earning a raise, bonus, or promotion. Those who have accountability partners add *social-level motivators* to the reasons they want to achieve their goal.

In your success journal, make a check mark next to everything in your *Want It List* that could be classified as a social-level motivator.

The problem with doing things at these levels of motivation is you likely don't *want* to do them. When opposition arises or depression hits (more about that in Chapter 9), all of your consequence- and social-level motivators will fall by the wayside.

If your *Want It List* comprises mostly consequence- or social-level motivators, you are likely going to feel *stuck.*

This is especially true if you go through life *should-ing* on yourself.

A lot of people set goals simply because they believe they really "should" do better in certain areas of their lives.

"I really *should* wake up an hour earlier every morning."
"I really *should* get rid of those extra twenty pounds."
"I really *should* stop eating chocolate."
"I really *should* spend more time with my in-laws."
"I really *should* go to the gym."
"I really *should* be making prospecting calls right now."

The list could go on forever.

The problem is, any sentence that begins with "I really *should*" usually ends with "but I don't want to."

If you feel *stuck,* it may be because you are *should-ing* on yourself.

This creates conflict inside you. Part of you is motivated to do whatever it is, but another part of you would rather not.

This kind of motivation usually does not last, which is why most people quit their New Year's resolutions within a few weeks.

In your success journal, make a list of all the ways you *should on* yourself. Make this list as extensive and comprehensive as possible. Keep this list in mind as we discuss the next levels of motivation.

In your success journal, write the following statement in big, bold letters:

"THE ABUNDANT AND FULFILLING LIFE IS CREATED WHEN *SHOULDS* ARE REPLACED WITH *GENUINE DESIRES.*"

This brings us to the next level of motivation. We do things at an *agent level* simply because we genuinely *want* to.

The most successful people in the world do what they do because they absolutely *love* doing what they do. People become physically fit because they develop a passion for the process of becoming physically fit. They find nutrition and exercise plans they thoroughly enjoy, so they stick with them.

This is what made the difference for me in my fitness journey.

I struggled with my weight for years because I absolutely love food; I love cooking it, I love planning for it, and I love eating it. I plan vacations to theme parks around the restaurants we will be experiencing (isn't that ridiculous?). I believed the process of slimming down was one of deprivation, torture, and endless hours in the gym every day. So I never wanted to begin the process.

Chapter 3: Stay Motivated!

Can you relate?

Have you ever felt *stuck* because you desired a certain outcome but believed the process of reaching it would be more painful than the process of staying where you were?

Countless individuals want to quit their jobs and start a business. Unfortunately, they never do because they believe the process will be too "risky" and involve enormous amounts of struggle, so they keep their dead-end jobs. Countless individuals are dissatisfied with their relationships, but they never do anything to change their situation because they believe it will be more painful to be single again.

What if the process of change was extremely enjoyable?

What if you found ways to change and grow that were even more pleasurable than what you are currently experiencing?

These were the very questions I asked myself at the beginning of my fitness journey.

Was it possible to permanently slim down *without* deprivation, torture, and endless hours in the gym? What if I could continue to enjoy all the foods I love, found exercises I thoroughly enjoy doing, and could easily and effortlessly release the mental and emotional weight that comes with excess body fat? If I could, I wanted to know how, because that would be a plan I could stick to. That would be a plan I could turn into a new *lifestyle*, thus making my results *permanent*.

Thankfully, the answer was a resounding *yes!*

While this is not the place to recount my journey to releasing more than sixty-five pounds in five months, suffice it to say, I found a way to reach my fitness goals by doing things I *wanted* to do, thus allowing myself to act at an agent level of motivation. (If you would like a free copy of Total Body Transformation, simply email me at Eric@FeelWellLiveWell.com with the subject "Total Body Transformation". Let me know you've read the book and would like a copy of the audio training.)

Consider this concept for a moment: What are things you do simply because you want to? Do you eat ice cream because you are trying to avoid a punishment? Did your parents say to you, "You must eat your entire bowl of ice cream, or you will not get any broccoli"? Do you eat ice cream because you really "should" eat ice cream? Does your family "expect you" to eat an entire bowl of ice cream before you go to bed at night?

Of course not!

If you are anything like me, you eat ice cream because you genuinely *want* to eat ice cream. You enjoy it, so you eat it. (And yes, even with my leaner body, I still enjoy eating ice cream on a regular basis!)

Go through your *Want It List* and draw a star next to each reason that could be classified as an agent-level motivator.

How many agent-level motivators do you have compared to your consequence- and social-level motivators? If you feel *stuck,* my guess is your consequence- and social-level motivators outnumber your agent-level motivators.

The highest level of motivation is what is known as *charity*-level motivation, which is doing things out of a deep, pure love for others. We do things at a charity level because we genuinely want to serve people, including ourselves, out of that divine love.

This is what usually motivates loving mothers. Consider that for a moment. Why would anyone want to carry another human being inside their body for nine months, endure hours of possibly excruciating pain during the birthing process, and then spend several years sacrificing personal desires to be a mother? The answer is simple: she is acting at a charity level; she has a deep, unwavering love for her children and would do anything for them.

In your success journal, draw a heart next to everything that could be classified as a charity-level motivator.

One of the fastest ways to get unstuck is to replace your consequence- and social-level motivators with agent- and charity-level motivators. If you are 100 percent willing and ready to do so, I invite you to participate in a

Chapter 3: Stay Motivated!

visualization exercise. To do so, you need to be somewhere you can concentrate without being disturbed.

Ready?

In your mind, see yourself walking down a path. This represents the path of your life. As you continue down this path, you notice that it forks. You must make a choice between taking the path to the left or taking the path to the right.

The path to the left is a path of ease. It is a downhill path where there are no obstacles, no challenges, and where no change or growth is required. Taking this path means simply continuing to do exactly what you have always done.

The path to the right is an uphill path. It requires change and progress. You will have to overcome many obstacles and challenges. This is the path that leads to growth reward.

In your mind, see yourself choosing the path to the left. Again, this path is easy. It requires no change, no growth, and no progress. Imagine yourself continuing down this path for one whole year. Project yourself, in your mind, one year into the future; one full year of taking this path to the left. This means one full year of making zero changes, experiencing zero growth and zero progress. You have spent zero time outside your comfort zone. Instead, you have continued to do exactly what you have been doing for another year. In your mind, look around you and notice what your life is like now. See what you see, hear what you hear, and feel what you feel one year into the future, one year of continuing to take this path to the left.

What is your life like?

How does that feel?

Now project yourself ten years into the future, having continued down this path to the left. This means ten more years of making zero changes, experiencing zero growth and zero progress. Notice what your life is like now. See what you see, hear what you hear, and feel what you feel ten years into the future, ten full years of continuing down this path to the left.

What is your life like now?

How does that feel?

Now project yourself, in your mind, all the way to the end of your mortal life. Imagine yourself on your deathbed, having continued down this path to the left for the rest of your life. Go there in your mind and notice what your life has become—having made zero changes, zero growth, and zero progress. See what you see, hear what you hear, and feel what you feel at the end of your mortal life of continuing down this path to the left.

What has become of your life?

How does that feel?

What is it like knowing you took the easy way out for the rest of your life?

Because you chose this path, you did not reach your highest potential and were not able to serve all the lives you were sent here to serve. In your mind, see all the people whom you were supposed to serve, but did not, surrounding your death bed. Imagine that one of them steps forward to act as spokesperson for the entire group. In your mind, hear the message they have for you at the end of your mortal life, having continued down the path to the left instead of serving all these people.

In your success journal, write this message down and read it out loud to yourself.

This is what you can expect if you choose the path to the left.

Thankfully, you always have a choice.

Now imagine that you are back at the fork in the road, looking at the two paths. This time you take the path to the right. Again, this is an uphill path. It requires change and progress. You will have to overcome many obstacles and challenges. This is the path that leads to growth, achievement, and reward. This is the path that leads to reaching your full potential and becoming your greatest and highest self.

Imagine yourself continuing up this path for one whole year. Project yourself, in your mind, one year into the future. This means one full year of change, growth, progress, and rewards. You have overcome many obstacles and achieved an entire year of goals. In your mind, look around you and notice what your life is like now. See what you see, hear what you hear, and feel what you feel one year into the future, one full year of continuing to take the path to the right.

What is your life like?

How does that feel?

Now project yourself, in your mind, ten years into the future, having continued on this path to the right. This means ten more years of change, growth, progress, and rewards. You have overcome even greater obstacles and achieved an entire decade of goals. In your mind, notice what your life is like now. See what you see, hear what you hear, and feel what you feel ten years into the future, ten full years of continuing up the path to the right.

What is your life like now?

How does that feel?

Now project yourself, one more time, all the way to the end of your mortal life. Imagine yourself on your deathbed, having continued up this path to the right for the rest of your life. You have truly transformed into your greatest and highest self. You have achieved everything you set out to achieve. Go there in your mind and notice what your life has become after a lifetime of change, growth, progress, and rewards. See what you see, hear what you hear, and feel what you feel at the end of your mortal life, having continued up this path to the right.

What has become of your life?

How does that feel?

Because you chose this path, you reached your highest potential and were able to serve all the lives you were sent here to serve. In your mind, see your posterity and all the people you served surrounding your deathbed to pay their final respects and thank you for all you did for them. See the gratitude and appreciation in their countenances for the choices you made and the impact those choices had on them. Imagine one of them steps forward to act as spokesperson for the entire group. In your mind, hear the message they have for you.

Write this message down in your success journal, and read it out loud to yourself.

This is what you can expect if you choose the path to the right.

Now imagine yourself passing from this life into the next and being greeted by the Divine. The Divine embraces you and welcomes you, saying, "Well done, thou good and faithful servant. You did so well. You did everything I asked you to do." Imagine the Divine's hand being placed over your heart, filling you with pure, celestial white light and love. This love fills every part of your being in such a way that all the reasons on your *Don't Want It List* simply melt away. There is no more room to contain those reasons, for you are completely filled with pure, divine love; there is no room for anything else. This pure, celestial white light and love permeate your very body, mind, and soul, emanating from every part of you.

Breathe that love in now.

What does that feel like?

This love is now a permanent part of you. Allow it to be the defining factor in all of your decisions from now on.

Keep this love in mind as you consider which path to take each day.

Now that you are filled with this divine light and pure love, you may find that you have several more agent- and charity-level reasons to add to your *Want It List*. Write these reasons down in your success journal.

Next, turn all of your agent- and charity-level reasons into declarations, post them on your bedroom or office wall, and read them out loud to yourself each day. This will keep you driven and your spirits high.

Now place your hand over your heart and declare, "I am amazing!"

"Eric, how do I make sure I stay on the path to the right?"

The key to staying on the path to the right is tapping into *inspiration* and *visualization*.

CHAPTER 4
INSPIRATION BLOCKERS

Have you ever awakened in the middle of the night and simply could not go back to sleep regardless of how hard you tried?

My wife and I made plans to celebrate Easter with my family in California a number of years ago.

"I can't wait to go," I told her. "I'll get to see my aunts, uncles, and some of the cousins I haven't seen in several years. This is going to be great!"

As the holiday drew closer, I awakened one night with a strong feeling that we were not to leave town.

"That doesn't make sense," I thought. "We've been trying to get together with my family for years, and this is the perfect time to do so. Why *wouldn't* we go to California for Easter?"

Suddenly, I remembered a conference being held near our home the Friday and Saturday before Easter. We had participated in this conference in previous years and always had a great experience, but we hadn't registered this time because of our plans to travel to California. The more I thought about the conference, the stronger I felt pressed to register for it.

Does this ever happen to you? Do you ever feel strongly pressed to take some sort of action even though it doesn't seem to make logical sense?

Following the prompting, I contacted the person in charge of the conference and asked if she had any space left in the vendor area. She did, so I promptly paid her the vendor fee. When the day arrived, I drove to the conference building and set up shop. Thousands were attending this weekend conference, and many of them would pass my table. I would have the chance to introduce them to my business and the services we provide in hope of gaining new clients.

Several hours passed, and I didn't seem to be getting anywhere. Conference attendees were more interested in buying the cookies, cakes, and brownies other vendors provided than they were in investing in changing their lives.

Then a young woman in her mid-twenties walked by our booth and stopped to talk to us. We found out she made very little money at her job, struggled with several health challenges, felt lonely and unfulfilled in her life, and was on a career path her parents wanted her to pursue. Unwilling to cause turmoil within her family, she followed their advice even though she didn't enjoy it. She had always dreamed of helping people heal, utilizing a technique similar to what she saw her chiropractor do, but she felt *stuck*.

She was the reason we felt compelled to be at that conference and miss celebrating Easter with my family.

Over the course of the next eighteen months, this young woman registered for every program and service my company offered, including certifying in the healthcare technique my company uses in our clinics; transformed into a gifted mentor and trainer; overcame her health challenges; attracted and married the man of her dreams; and settled into a fulfilling and lucrative career as a full-time healthcare practitioner. None of this would have happened had my wife and I ignored the prompting to be at that conference.

Many people get *stuck* in life because they fail to act on divine *inspiration*.

Chapter 4: Inspiration Blockers

Inspiration often comes in unexpected ways, and often it won't seem to make logical sense.

My wife and I were on our way to a religious temple near our home where we go to meditate and feel closer to the Divine. As we parked our car, I was suddenly overcome with a powerful impression that we needed to be somewhere else.

"Heather," I said, "this doesn't make any sense, but I feel very strongly that this isn't the place we are supposed to be right now."

"What do you mean?" she asked, her voice reflecting the same confusion she heard in mine. "This is the temple! How could this *not* be the place we're supposed to be?"

"I have no idea," was my response. "I just feel like we need to go somewhere else."

"Where would we go?"

As if someone else were using my voice, I replied, "Let's go get a couple's massage!"

My wife looked at me as if I had gone completely mad, but she trusted me and simply responded, "If it's right, what else matters?"

As we finished our couple's massage and were in the lobby getting ready to pay, my wife recognized a gentleman with whom she had attended school. After they exchanged pleasantries, she remembered that she and I were hosting a couples' retreat in our home just a few days later and needed a massage therapist to give massages to those attending. Up to that point, all other massage therapists we had spoken to had been unavailable.

He readily accepted the position.

While at my home, he struck up a conversation with one of the mentors who worked for my company and found they had a lot in common. The massage therapist signed up to be a mentee with our company in order to achieve several goals. He had been *stuck*, but, because we were willing to follow inspiration when it didn't seem to make sense, this gentleman was able to get unstuck and find more fulfillment in life than he had experienced before.

"But, Eric, how do I know if it really is inspiration and not some crazy thought that pops into my mind?"

I'm glad you asked because the answer is actually quite simple: Our own thoughts tend to go to our *brains*, while inspiration tends to go to our *hearts.*

When seemingly random impressions come to you, check your feelings. If no feeling accompanies the thought, it is likely it was nothing more than a thought. If there is a feeling, it is likely you are receiving inspiration.

Inspiration that encourages me to take specific action steps is often accompanied by feelings of peace, joy, excitement, and urgency, while inspiration that encourages me to avoid certain things is accompanied by an unsettling feeling. It is important to note that fear is *not* a feeling that accompanies true inspiration, although it can often *follow* true inspiration. It is not uncommon for someone to feel pressed to do something, feel peaceful and excited about doing it, and then feel "attacked" by fear, so he doesn't end up doing it.

There is an opposing force in the world that does not want us to be happy and successful. For the purpose of this book, we will simply refer to this force as *opposition*. Opposition uses fear and doubt to dissuade us from taking action that will lead us to greater heights.

Whenever new clients sign up for one of my top-level mentoring programs, I tell them in no uncertain terms that they will likely face intense opposition in the coming weeks. They might face fear and doubt as they never have before.

Some people give in to the fear. They choose to back out of commitments they make to themselves and immediately feel a "relief" from the opposition, which they then use as justification for backing out.

Chapter 4: Inspiration Blockers

"I knew that program wasn't right for me," they proclaim. "As soon as I backed out of it, I immediately felt better!"

What they don't realize is the reason they felt better was because the opposition let up because the opposition won. Opposition caused them to back out of the commitment that would have led them to new heights and greater levels of joy and fulfillment had they followed through. Opposition wants people to be miserable, complacent, and *stuck*, so it attacks shortly after commitments are made.

As you learned in Chapter 2, you will encounter opposition in phase three of your success cycle after accepting the call and passing through the honeymoon phase. Fear is one of the biggest causes of getting *stuck*. Don't worry; you will learn how to overcome fear in Chapter 5.

"But, Eric, how can you tell if inspiration is coming from the Divine rather than from opposition?"

Again, the answer is quite simple. If you feel inspired to do good, the inspiration is likely coming from the Divine. If you feel inspired to do something not so good, it is likely coming from opposition. Again, consult with your feelings. If you feel peaceful, excited, joyful, and/or a sense of urgency as you consider taking the action, take the action. If you feel unsettled (not to be confused with fear), do not take the action.

Another mistake some people make is thinking they need to know every part of the journey before beginning.

As part of our Valentine's Day celebration a number of years ago, I presented my wife with a card explaining that a number of special gifts waited for her and our children around the house. They would need to follow a set of clues to find the next gift. The first clue was inside the card. They read the clue and took immediate action to find their first gift. This was accompanied by another clue, which led to another gift, and another clue—and so on, until they finally found their "ultimate Valentine's Day gift": a forty-ounce box of gourmet chocolates.

Inspiration often comes one piece at a time, meaning the second step of the journey isn't revealed until you take the first step. Some people choose to discredit the source of inspiration when they can't see the entire course of action from the very beginning.

Have you ever driven down a dark road at night? Could you see the entire road at once? Probably not. As long as you had working headlights, you were able to see enough of the road to stay on it until you reached your destination. The next hundred feet or so were illuminated every second that passed as you continued moving forward. You could drive thousands of miles in this manner. It isn't necessary to see the whole journey before you begin. As long as you continue moving forward and have working headlights, the next step of your journey will become visible at the appropriate time.

The same is true of inspiration. We are often given one step at a time. As long as we take that step, we will be led to another, and then to another, until we reach our destination and achieve the goal.

Unfortunately, most people have *inspiration blockers*. If you find it difficult to receive inspiration, it is likely you are experiencing at least one of the following:

1) **No higher power.** There are some people who outright refuse to believe in any sort of higher power. These are the extreme intellectuals who believe that, if something cannot be explained using visible scientific evidence, it must not exist.

   One of my mentors shared an experience he had with one of his clients. Part of his mentoring program included choosing and following a higher power. When the mentor asked the client what he called his higher power, the client responded that he didn't have one.

   "You need to have a higher power as part of this program," the mentor explained.

Chapter 4: Inspiration Blockers

"But why?" was the response. "I'm a suit and tie kind of guy. I don't have time to believe in any sort of fictional 'higher power.' "

"Trust me," the mentor continued. "A time will come when you feel *stuck*. In that moment, you will need to have access to inspiration to know how to get unstuck. Choose something that is bigger than you to be your higher power."

"Fine," the client responded sarcastically. Pointing out the window, "I choose that mountain as my higher power."

"Great," the mentor said.

"You can't be serious," the client continued. "What am I supposed to do now?"

"Any time you feel stuck, talk to your higher power and ask for guidance."

"You want me to talk to a mountain?" the client asked skeptically.

"Yep!"

Several weeks passed before their next appointment. When the time of the appointment arrived, the client sat down, crossed his arms, and glared at the mentor.

"Tell me what has happened since our last appointment," the mentor began.

"Oh, you *know* what happened," the client retorted.

"You have my attention," the mentor replied. "Please tell me."

With a large, reluctant sigh, the client explained, "Well, I was in a sales meeting last week. My team and I were meeting with representatives from a large company regarding a deal that, if closed, would bring more revenue than any other deal before it. Unfortunately, the meeting wasn't going well, and it didn't look like we were going to close the deal."

He gulped before continuing. "We took a quick restroom break, and on my way back into the conference room, I glanced out the window and saw "my" mountain. 'Okay, Mr. Mountain,' I thought. 'Mr. Higher Power, what am I supposed to do?' "

At this point, he stopped talking and just glared at the mentor.

"What happened next?" the mentor asked.

"Well..." the client hesitated. "You never told me the mountain was going to speak back to me."

With a large smile, the mentor nudged, "And?"

Reluctantly the client continued. "As soon as I asked the question, a clear idea of what I needed to do and say came to my mind. We went back into the conference room, I did and said what I felt impressed to do and say, and we ended up closing the deal. I couldn't believe it!"

If you do not currently have a higher power, get one. They're free!

Answer the following question in your success journal:

My higher power is _____.

You could call your higher power whatever you choose. I call my higher power God or Heavenly Father. You could call yours Universe, Higher Self, Source Energy, whatever is in tune with your personal beliefs.

Write the following in your success journal:

"I always look to my higher power for guidance and inspiration."

Now place your hand over your heart and declare, "I am amazing!"

2) **Failing to write inspiration down.** Have you ever received a potentially life-changing idea but failed to write it down, so you ended up forgetting it? I often receive ideas as I'm about to fall asleep, when the house is quiet and everything is still. Does this ever happen to you? Have you ever made the mistake of thinking you'll remember the idea the next morning, only to find that it was gone when you woke up?

I like to imagine there is an inspiration department in heaven that is extremely generous when it comes to ideas that, if imple-

Chapter 4: Inspiration Blockers

mented, will allow people to grow and progress. Unfortunately, most people make the mistake of failing to write ideas down the moment they receive them. When the inspiration department sees someone being a poor steward over the ideas sent, it stops sending that person ideas. Instead, it sends the ideas to those who *do* write them down and implement them.

If you read biographies of the greatest minds in history, you will notice a pattern; they all kept something with them to write down ideas as soon as they received them. For some, this meant carrying a small notebook that could fit into their pocket. Those of us who live in the twenty-first century have a better tool: smartphones.

Whenever an idea comes to my mind, I email it to myself. The subject line is whatever project it pertains to. For example, whenever I read or heard a principle I wanted to include in this book, I immediately opened my email application, typed "Being Stuck Sucks, So Stop It!" as the subject, and emailed the principle to myself. When the time came for me to actually write this book, I simply accessed my Sent mail and searched "Being Stuck Sucks, So Stop It!" All of the ideas I had for this book came up. I copied and pasted them into a single document, organized them, and expanded on each idea.

Emailing your ideas to yourself is a great way to keep them organized because you do not have to search through pages of notes to find individual ideas. This is also helpful if you have young children who could play with or misplace your notebook. When you email your ideas to yourself, you can access them nearly anywhere.

Do not make the mistake of procrastinating. Sometimes, the best ideas are lost after only a few minutes. When ideas come, write them down *immediately.*

Write the following in your success journal:

"I immediately write my ideas down."

Now place your hand over your heart and declare, "I am amazing!"

3) **Failing to act on inspiration.** Have you noticed that ideas for world-changing inventions seem to go to multiple people at once? If you look through history, you will find that several people had the idea for the printing press, the telephone, the light bulb, the automobile, the airplane, and more. So how come only one or two people are credited for each invention?

The inspiration department knows how important these world-changing inventions are, so they send ideas to several people at once in hopes at least one of them will take action and implement the ideas.

If you fail to receive inspiration, maybe you received inspiration in the past but failed to act on it. If the inspiration department knows you won't act regardless of how valuable the ideas are, it will stop sending them to you. Instead, it will send them to someone who *will* act.

"But what if the idea doesn't seem to make sense?"

It often won't.

"But that isn't logical!"

It may seem that way to you now because you do not currently have the logic someone at the level you hope to achieve has. This is why it is impossible to "logic" your way to new levels of success. It wasn't "logical" for my wife and me to register for the conference instead of going to California for Easter, but we did it anyway, and we reaped the reward. It wasn't "logical" to invest nearly $5,000 in a mentoring program while we were still on welfare, but we did it anyway, and we reaped the reward.

Write the following in your success journal:

Chapter 4: Inspiration Blockers

"After writing ideas down, I always do them, even if they don't seem to make sense."

Now place your hand over your heart and declare, "I am amazing!"

4) **Your mind is too full to receive any more.** Do you ever feel overwhelmed? Do you ever feel like your brain is overloaded? Do you find yourself constantly tired even though you get enough sleep and eat a healthy diet?

   It is possible your life is filled with too much clutter, chaos, and disorganization. Or, you may simply have so much information and so many ideas, there is no room in your brain for more.

   Imagine the mind is like a silver platter, and ideas and inspiration are manna from heaven. If the platter is never emptied, regardless how large, it will eventually become full and unable to hold any more. As important as it is to continue learning and furthering your education, if you never do anything to *reset* your mind, eventually you will run out of room in it.

   How do you *reset* your mind?

Trying to remember things requires a significant amount of energy. Creating a *procrastination list* frees that energy, allowing you to put it toward other, more useful things.

In your success journal, make a list of everything you have been procrastinating. Make this list as extensive as possible. Then create a plan of action for accomplishing everything on your list. Set specific dates and times for getting each item done, and then make sure to do them. Checking items off your procrastination list will free up room in your mind to receive inspiration, and keeping the commitments you set for completing each task will also give you a burst of energy. Each time you keep a commitment, your brain releases dopamine into your body, which gives you a feeling of motivation and creates a burst of energy, which can further help you get *unstuck*.

If, after creating and completing the tasks on your procrastination list, you still feel *stuck,* consider taking a *creation vacation.* This is a chance to get away, relax, rejuvenate, be in an abundant atmosphere, and allow your brain to create and receive ideas naturally. Some of my most lucrative ideas came from creation vacations I took with my wife.

Here are some guidelines for creation vacations:

1) Go with people who support what you do and can contribute ideas. This can include business partners, company executives, mentors, spouses, or whomever you feel would best contribute to the creation of ideas. I do *not* recommend taking young children on creation vacations.

2) Invest in food, lodging, and activities that promote a feeling of abundance. The more successful you feel during your vacation, the more successful ideas you will be able to create. This is *not* the time to be cheap.

3) Take a notebook or another tool to capture ideas as they come to you. Even if the ideas don't seem to make sense, immediately write them down.

4) Allow ideas to flow naturally. Don't try to force them. When you put yourself in a state of creation, ideas will come.

The *AWDRR* Principle

In order to achieve large, long-term goals, you must take regular action steps toward those goals. To know what action steps to take will require personally communicating with your higher power on a daily basis. If you are like me, this may take place during a morning and evening prayer. If your higher power is the universe or a higher self, this may take place during meditation or while spending time in nature. Whatever method you personally use to tap into inspiration, make sure to do it as you apply the *AWDRR principle*.

AWDRR is an acronym for Ask, Write, Do, Report, Receive the Reward. One of the first things you do as you get out of bed in the morning is communicate with your higher power. Ask for specific action steps to accomplish that day. Do not end your prayer or meditation until something comes to mind. The action step may not make sense, but *do not discard it*. As long as it is legal, moral, and ethical (which of course it will be when coming from your higher power), there is a purpose in your achieving it. *Immediately* write it down. *Never* try to simply remember your action step without writing it down.

You may receive more than one action step per day. If you receive multiple action steps during this process, write them all down and make sure to accomplish them all before you go to bed that night.

The next step, of course, is to *do* whatever you feel pressed to do. Again, it may not seem logical. Do it anyway. Your action step may lead you down a different, yet faster, path to achieving your goal.

One word of caution: make sure you aren't simply writing down and doing "busy work" instead of inspired action steps. There may be times when you feel compelled to take a certain action step, but you choose not to write it down and complete it because it doesn't make sense or you fear completing it. It might be outside your comfort zone, so you write down some kind of *busy work* instead of *inspired action steps*. Things such as going for a walk or doing your dishes. You may even feel justified in doing such menial tasks because they keep you busy, but they may not propel you toward your goal.

That doesn't mean going for a walk or doing your dishes can't be an inspired action step. The purpose in this is to actually tap into inspiration to know how to continue moving forward.

At night, you get to have another conversation with your higher power, this time to report your progress. If you completed your action steps, great!

You get to report that you got them done, and you are now ready to *receive the reward* that comes from doing so. Sometimes the reward is more action steps—another piece of the puzzle. Sometimes the reward is a blissful feeling of accomplishment. Few prayers are more fulfilling than those that include the words, "I completed the work I was given today." Sometimes you find that completing your action steps led you to accomplish the goal you set for yourself. And yes, sometimes the reward can even be financial. I can't tell you how many times I have felt pressed to complete a certain action step only to find myself $50,000 richer the next day.

If you fail to complete an action step, ask your higher power for forgiveness for failing to be a good steward over the inspiration you received. You may not receive further action steps until you complete the ones you have procrastinated. Be patient with yourself. Remember your goal is *progress*, not *perfection*.

Write the following in your success journal:

"Each day, I ask my higher power for specific action steps. When I receive them, I immediately write them down, then do them before the end of the day. At night, I report back to my higher power that I completed my action steps and then receive my reward."

Now place your hand over your heart and declare, "I am amazing!"

You may have areas of your life that need to be cleaned up. If you struggle to receive inspiration, something in your life may be disconnecting you from the Source of inspiration. There may be commitments you failed to keep. You may be doing things contrary to your spiritual beliefs. Each of these can keep a person from receiving regular inspiration.

In your success journal, make a list of anything that may be out of alignment in your life. Next to each item, write a clear path of action you commit to taking to get this area of your life cleaned up, along with a date by which to get it done. With every area of your life you clean up, you will feel less and less *stuck*.

The more you do to release inspiration blockers, the more inspiration you will receive. Inspiration often comes at unexpected times, but are there ways to tap into inspiration *anytime* you need it? Are there ways to receive answers *anytime* you feel *stuck*?

Yes!

The following are tools you can utilize anytime you need answers:

Journal Prompts

Putting pen to paper is like unlocking the gates of the subconscious mind. The subconscious mind holds the answers to all things. It is simply a matter of accessing it to receive those answers.

One of my private mentoring clients was recently having a hard time overcoming a particularly difficult trial. She battled resentment toward certain men in her life, and she was unconsciously pushing money away. This showed up in the amount of money, or lack thereof, she was making in her business, as well as in other areas of her personal life. People—women especially—store three things in the same file in their subconscious minds: men, God, and money. Typically, if someone has had a negative experience with one of them, to one degree or another, they will push away the other two.

I invited my client to write out a number of journal prompts, leaving space in between each one for answers, including:

The reason(s) for me going through this trial include…

The lesson(s) I am to learn include…

This will ultimately serve me and be to my benefit because…

I invited her to write down the first things that came to mind after reading each prompt.

The first things that come to your mind often seem not to make sense: answers directly from the subconscious mind are rarely logical, but that doesn't make them any less true.

My client ended up writing down amazing answers, which gave her the perspective she was looking for. She realized that men weren't her enemy, that the trial she was facing was actually a blessing in disguise, and that she no longer needed to push money or her husband away from her.

Can you guess what happened?

Up until this point, she had been struggling for months to attract a single new client into her business. I received a text from her later that evening informing me that, within three hours of our mentoring appointment, she closed a $30,000 client. Thirty thousand dollars within three hours of her breakthrough—all because she wrote down a series of journal prompts and allowed herself to put pen to paper, writing down whatever came to her mind. Journal prompts are among the most effective tools for finding answers.

The Mirror Exercise

Some people find journaling difficult. They tend to find visualization exercises easier than writing exercises. If this is the case with you, start by clearing your mind. Take a few deep breaths in and exhale through your mouth to become fully present. In your mind, see a full-length mirror. In the mirror, picture your greatest and highest self, the one who has all experience, all knowledge, all wisdom, and can answer any and all questions regarding your greatest and highest good. Then pose whatever questions you may have out loud and speak the first answers that come to your mind. For example, if you are struggling to find your next step toward achieving a particular goal, ask, "Highest self, what is my next step?" Then speak whatever comes to your mind first. Do not stop to think about it. Do not discount what comes to your mind. Simply speak what comes to you.

Fifty Ways

Use this exercise to find ways to achieve a seemingly impossible goal. Just as the name implies, make a list of fifty different ways to achieve the goal. For example, years ago, when I needed to come up with $100,000 in seven days, something I had never done at that time, I made a list of anything that came to mind on how to do so. Several of the answers were ridiculous. They included such things as rob a bank; sell a kidney; create an abstract painting, claim it's an original Pollock, and sell it on eBay—things I would never actually do. What this did, however, was open my mind to possibilities and allow creative juices to flow. Pretty soon, after I had written ten to twenty ridiculous answers, I began to think of ways that would actually work. Seven days later, I manifested the money I needed.

Number a piece of paper from one to fifty (or to one hundred if you want to be extra ambitious), and write down any idea that comes to you, regardless of how crazy it seems. Writing an idea down doesn't mean you need to do it; you are simply coming up with possibilities for now. Real ideas will start to come once you have written a certain number of ridiculous ideas. Next, cross anything off your list that isn't legal, moral, and ethical, then narrow your list to what you feel are the top ten or twenty ideas. Put them in the chronological order you feel is best to take action on them, and commit to getting them done by a specific date and time. You now have a clearly laid-out plan for how to achieve your goal.

Eye Exercise

You may have heard that the eyes are the windows to the soul. They are also the windows to finding answers.

Have you ever asked someone how to do something that seemed impossible? I sometimes do this at my seminars. I choose a member of the audience who has never earned $25,000 in a single month and ask how he or she will generate $25,000 within the next seven days. The audience member usually thinks about the question for a moment and then responds, "I don't know."

If the rest of the audience is paying attention, they usually catch what happens.

Whenever you pose a question that someone has never considered before, their eyes ususally wander. Sometimes they glance up, sometimes they glance to the right, other times they look down for a second and then up and to the left.

The subconscious mind is looking for answers.

Imagine the mind is like a library with a book on every imaginable subject and an answer to any imaginable question. The eyes are the mind's librarians. When someone is asked a question to which she does not consciously have an answer, her "librarians" go directly to the part (or parts) of the mind's library where the "book" containing the answer is found. What happens most of the time is the person subconsciously finds the answer and rejects it because the answer seems illogical, difficult, or scary, so she responds with, "I don't know."

Anytime you feel *stuck* and in need of answers to a particularly difficult question or circumstance, invite a trusted friend or loved one to pose a specific question to you, such as, "How are you going to solve this problem?" or "How are you going to achieve X goal?" Once the individual poses the question, take three to five minutes to silently ponder the question while allowing your eyes to wander freely and naturally, wherever they want to go. Ask your partner to chart where your eyes go. For example, if they go up and to the right, ask your partner to take note of that. If they go down, to take note of that as well. Once the time has passed, ask your partner to go through your eye movements with you. Thank your partner for his or her help. That person's job is now complete.

The rest will be up to you.

Hold your eyes in each of the positions your eyes went during the three to five minutes, one at a time, while posing the question to yourself over and over again until at least one answer comes to mind. Immediately write the answer down. Ask yourself if there are any more answers that need to come from that eye position. If intuition tells you "yes," keep your eyes in the same position and continue to pose the question to yourself until you feel all answers from that "book" have been revealed. Repeat the process with all eye positions that your partner documented. Once you have all answers written down (these will usually be specific action steps to take), intuitively put them in the order you need to accomplish them. You now have a clear set of instructions on how to achieve your seemingly impossible goal.

Please keep in mind the following as you do these exercises:

1) The answers you seek must pertain directly to you or someone/something you have stewardship over. If you are not the president of the United States, you will not receive answers regarding how to fix certain areas of the United States only the president is capable of fixing. You will not receive answers to questions such as, "What is the exact date my next door neighbor's baby will be born?"

2) The answers you seek must be relevant to what you specifically need in that moment. For example, you likely will not receive answers to things several years into the future.

3) The answers you seek must be legal, moral, and ethical. These exercises will not work if you ask for other people's credit card information or how to effectively commit a crime. They will also not work for any form of gambling, such as asking for winning lottery ticket numbers.

What do you do if you receive inspiration to do something you don't want to do? What do you do if you receive action steps that seem scary or overwhelming? What if you feel pressed to take a major leap of faith that requires you to change your very nature?

There was once a young girl who accompanied her mother to the store. While shopping, the young girl's eyes fell upon a plastic pearl necklace, and she immediately fell in love with it.

"Please, Mommy," she begged. "Can we get this plastic pearl necklace? I love it so much! I'll have so much fun playing with it!"

The mother didn't have a lot of extra money but came up with a plan for the daughter to earn the necklace by doing extra chores around the house. The daughter readily agreed.

The day finally came that she was able to buy the plastic pearl necklace, and she was as happy as she could be.

From that moment on, she did everything while wearing her necklace. She played with her friends while wearing it, she bathed while wearing it, she slept while wearing it. She loved it so much she never wanted to take it off.

One evening, her father came home from work, walked into her room, and sat next to her on the bed. As usual, she was playing happily with the necklace wrapped around her neck.

"Daughter, do you love me?" he asked.

Surprised by the question, she responded, "Of course I love you. You know that. Why would you ask me such a thing?"

Looking her square in the eyes, her father replied, "My sweet daughter. I love you. I need you to give me your necklace."

Chapter 4: Inspiration Blockers

Shocked, she stared at him for several moments.

With tears in her eyes, she finally cried, "Daddy, you know how much I love this necklace. Why would you ask me to do such a thing? I have a Barbie doll. Do you want it instead?"

"No, my sweet girl," the father replied. "I need you to give me your necklace."

Holding back more tears, the daughter responded, "I'm sorry, Daddy, but I love the necklace too much. I cannot give it to you."

The father left.

The following evening, the father came home from work, walked into his daughter's room, and again sat on her bed next to her. Again, she was playing happily with the necklace wrapped around her neck.

"Daughter, do you love me?"

"Of course I love you," came the reply. "You know that. Why would you ask me such a thing?"

"My sweet daughter. I love you. I need you to give me your necklace."

Again, she stared at him for several moments before beginning to cry.

"Daddy, you know how much I love this necklace. Why would you ask me to do such a thing? I have a wristwatch. Do you want it instead?"

"No, my sweet girl," the father replied. "I need you to give me your necklace. Trust me."

"I'm sorry, Daddy, but I love the necklace too much. I cannot give it to you."

Once again, the father left.

For the third consecutive night, the father came home from work and walked into his daughter's room. This time he found her sitting on the edge of her bed sobbing. The plastic pearl necklace rested gently in her hands.

When she heard her father enter, she looked at him.

With great tears pouring down her cheeks, she cried, "Daddy, I don't understand why you've asked me to give you my necklace. You know how much I love it, but I love you even more, and I trust you, so please take it."

Solemnly, he grabbed the plastic pearl necklace and put it in his left pocket. From his right pocket, he pulled out a necklace of genuine pearls.

With tears of his own and a proud smile on his face, he exclaimed, "My sweet daughter, this is for you, for your trust in me and your obedience."

Is it possible you have been clinging to plastic pearl necklaces when you could be receiving genuine pearls?

Answer the following in your success journal:

The "plastic pearl necklaces" I have been clinging to include...

This is affecting me in the following ways...

As you learned in Chapter 2, it is usually right before the reward comes that fears and doubts are the strongest, making the temptation to cling to plastic pearl necklaces the strongest.

I struggled with my weight for many years. Every time I made a small amount of progress, I would plateau, lose motivation, and gain the weight back. At a networking meeting I attended, I met a gentleman who had won twenty-one world body-building championships, including Mr. Natural Universe, Mr. Natural Olympia, and Mr. Natural World. I decided to hire him as my personal trainer.

That was when the "freak-out" began.

Despite having plenty of funds in the bank, I found my mind playing tricks on me. For weeks, any time my wife informed me of an unexpected expense, I freaked out, even if the cost was only a few hundred dollars. As hard as I tried to overcome my fears, I struggled with the idea of paying this particular mentor the thousands of dollars he charged for six months of personal training. So I put it off.

Thankfully, like any good mentor or trainer will, this gentleman called me on it.

"Eric," he said. "It's normal, right before making a life-changing commitment, for you to experience fears and doubts."

My mind immediately responded with, "Eric, don't you teach people this?"

He was right. I recommitted, paid him in full, and signed up for his training program.

That evening, I received a very strong impression; if I wanted to fully transform, I needed to overcome the emotional issues that caused me to put on a lot of the excess weight in the first place. Much of my emotional "baggage" stemmed from being adopted as an infant. I believed I was adopted because my biological parents didn't want me. I had never met them nor did I know who they were or where they lived.

The thought came to me to hire a private investigator to locate them. I did, and seven days later, I received an email with my biological mother's contact information and a link to her social media page. I reached out and was finally able to meet my biological parents, five siblings I never knew I had, and several other family members, including a living great grandmother. None of that would have happened had I clung to my "plastic pearl necklace" and given in to my fear about hiring the personal trainer.

I learned a long time ago to simply trust my gut instinct and take immediate action. I don't know of a single person who said, "You know what? I went with my gut feeling, and boy, do I regret it!"

When you follow inspiration, things *always* work out. Perhaps not in the way you expect them to, but they *always* work out.

"But, Eric, what if I do follow my gut, and something bad happens?"

If you follow inspiration and something "bad" happens, it is usually because you've done one of the following:

1) You may have deviated from the path you were inspired to take. Perhaps you felt pressed to do something a certain way. Perhaps you did it 90 percent the way you felt pressed to do it and 10 percent your own way, causing a different result to come into your life.

2) You may not have been on your perfect path, and the "bad thing" happened so you would get back on it.

Larry H. Miller was one of the most prominent businessmen in Utah. He was an active member of The Church of Jesus Christ of Latter-day Saints. As such, he was expected to follow the biblically established practice of paying a tithe to the church of 10 percent of his income in exchange for the blessings outlined in the Bible. During an interview with one of his religious leaders, he was asked if he tithed, and he said no. He couldn't explain why he didn't; as a successful businessman, it was never a question of money. So he committed to doing so.

He was working at the time as a regional manager over a number of car dealerships. Within sixty days of beginning to tithe, he was demoted.

"This can't be right," he thought. "The Bible promises extra *blessings* when we pay our tithing, and I've just been demoted. This seems like a step backward."

The demotion persuaded him to quit working for that company and start his own dealership. Doing so increased his income significantly. He first experienced what he thought was a major setback, but doing so led him to his perfect path, and he became a multimillionaire.

Write down the following phrase in your success journal:

"I'll think about it."

Once you do, cross it out. I invite you to completely eliminate this phrase from your vocabulary.

Napoleon Hill, author of *Think and Grow Rich* and *Outwitting the Devil*, says that unsuccessful people tend to be slow to make up their mind and quick to change it. They often use the phrase, "I'll think about it" to put off making important decisions or to avoid telling a person, "No, thank you."

Write the following in your success journal:

Chapter 4: Inspiration Blockers

"The phrase, 'I'll think about it' keeps people *stuck*!"

The longer it takes you to make decisions, the more *stuck* you will become. Those who sit around "thinking about things" usually don't take the *actions* necessary to create success.

We have already agreed there is an opposing force in the world that doesn't want us to become happy and successful. One of the tools that force uses is *indecision*. Consider that for a moment. The longer you take to make a decision, the more that opposing force influences that decision by putting fear and doubts into your mind.

On the flip side, Napoleon Hill says that successful people tend to be quick to make up their mind and slow to change it.

"So, Eric, are you encouraging me to make important decisions on a *whim*?"

No. It is important to gather the information you need and study the decision, but that does *not* mean the process has to take a long time.

Some of the most important decisions of my life were made in *seconds*. Opportunities presented themselves to me, I asked for the facts, weighed the pros and cons in my mind, and checked my intuition and feelings. If I did not feel right about proceeding, I simply said, "No, thank you," and moved on. If I felt peaceful about proceeding, I said, "Yes," and proceeded.

Just as important as it is to make decisions quickly, it is also important to *keep the commitments you make*. As we have already discussed, often shortly after you make a commitment to do something that will change your life for the better, opposition puts fears and doubts into your mind.

Write the following in your success journal:

"When major decisions are to be made, I quickly gather the information I need and check in with my intuition. If intuition tells me not to move forward, I simply say, 'No, thank you.' If intuition tells me to move forward, I say, 'Yes,' and stick with my commitment."

Now place your hand over your heart and declare, "I am amazing!"

"But, Eric, what if I make a decision quickly and then fail?"

There is a major difference between *failure* and *defeat*. Failure is actually part of success.

Consider infants learning to walk. The only way to do so is by stumbling, falling, and getting back up. Doing so strengthens the muscles in their legs and increases their coordination, making walking possible.

Write the following in your success journal:

"I make decisions quickly. I embrace failure. Failure is part of achieving success. When I fail, I get back up and try again."

Now place your hand over your heart and declare, "I am amazing!"

Defeat only happens when you stop trying. The biggest difference between someone who succeeds and someone who does not is the person who succeeds fails more times than the person who does not has even tried.

"But, Eric, what if I do everything you've suggested in this chapter, and I still don't feel like inspiration comes to me?"

If this is the case, *you* may actually be the inspiration blocker.

Have you ever blocked someone on your phone or on social media? It is possible you may have (figuratively) done this with the Source of Inspiration.

If you've done all the exercises in this chapter and still feel unable to receive inspiration, you may have had an experience that caused you to associate your higher power with pain. This may be the case if you have ever experienced abuse from a male authority figure, such as a father, grandfather, uncle, teacher, or religious leader. This may be the case if you have ever experienced what you thought was an unanswered prayer.

A friend of mine, whom I'll call Adam, recalled an experience when, as a young boy, he dreamed of owning a goldfish. His parents finally

Chapter 4: Inspiration Blockers

bought him one for his birthday. He was so thrilled he vowed to do everything he could to take excellent care of his goldfish.

As a member of a church-going family, Sunday came, and he said a prayer to ask God to please watch over and take care of his goldfish while he was at church.

When he returned home, to his horror, his goldfish was dead.

This gave him the impression that his higher power either didn't listen or didn't care about his prayer, which created a lot of resentment.

As he reflected on his life years later, he looked for ways to overcome his obstacles and realized he wasn't receiving inspiration as readily as he wanted to. He had created a barrier between himself and his higher power to keep him "protected" from the pain he felt as a child. Because of this mental barrier, he had "blocked" his higher power from freely communicating with him.

Can you relate? Is it possible you have constructed a mental or emotional barrier between you and your higher power that keeps inspiration from coming to you?

In your success journal, I invite you to write a letter to your higher power. If you call your higher power God, start the letter with "Dear God," if you call your higher power Heavenly Father, start the letter with "Dear Heavenly Father," and so on. Ask yourself if you have created any sort of barrier between you and your higher power. If so, what experience led you to do so? Once the experience (or experiences) come to mind, write about them in your letter. Don't worry, this is not sacrilegious in any way. This is simply a way to release toxic emotions, help you heal, and clear up the flow of inspiration.

When my friend did this exercise, his letter said something like, "Dear Heavenly Father,

We need to talk! Remember that goldfish I had? I asked You to please watch over it and keep it safe. And what happened? I came home from church (of all places) to find it dead! That made me so sad. How could such a thing happen? Why didn't You answer my prayer?

Love,

Adam"

Write your letter to your higher power in your success journal now and express whatever you feel needs to be expressed.

Once you've completed this task, take a quick break. Then write a response letter as if your higher power were writing back to you. Write down anything that comes to mind, even if it doesn't seem to make sense.

When my friend did this, it went something like,

"Dearest Adam,

Thank you for your letter. I know how sad you felt when you found your goldfish dead. Of course I heard and answered your prayer. The answer was simply a "no" because you needed to learn specific lessons, including the one you have learned today; that sometimes people block Me from talking to them. Please teach this principle to others. I am counting on you to be an instrument in My hands. Because of this lesson you have just learned, you will experience many great blessings. I love you more than words can express.

Your loving Heavenly Father."

As you write your response letter, you may receive words of counsel, understanding, and wisdom. You may come to see the experience you had from a different perspective.

Write your response letter now.

Once you have, read it to yourself out loud.

How does this change things?

Write the following in your success journal:

"Whenever I feel *stuck,* I tap into inspiration, receive answers, and take immediate action."

Now place your hand over your heart and declare, "I am amazing!

Chapter 4: Inspiration Blockers

Visualization

Just as inspiration blockers can keep you *stuck,* so too can *vision blockers*. Many fail to achieve their goals because they cannot *see* themselves achieving those goals.

Have you ever tried driving a car with a dirty windshield? Have you ever tried driving at night without headlights? I hope not, because doing so would be extremely dangerous. Unfortunately, many try to navigate through life with little or no vision of their goals.

In Utah, we get pretty heavy snow in the winter. If someone leaves a car outside and a snowstorm hits, he or she will likely find the windshield completely covered in ice, making it impossible to see through.

If you wanted to drive from point A to point B but found your windshield covered in ice, you would clear it before going anywhere.

The purpose of this chapter is to "clear your windshield" and give you clarity so that getting from point A to point B becomes easier. This will require a bit of imagination and a willingness to play along.

In your success journal, on the left side of a blank page, draw a picture of yourself. Next, on the right side of the page, draw a picture of everything you desire in life, such as riches, a healthy body, or relationships. Whatever it is you desire, draw it on the right side of the page. Finally, in the middle of the page, draw a barrier, or wall, separating you from all you desire.

Do you ever feel like you've hit a wall? Do you ever feel like something is keeping you from reaching a new level of success? This is quite common.

When subconscious walls stand between you and the things you desire in life, you will be unable to see yourself achieving them, and you will remain *stuck*.

Look closely at your drawing. Tapping into intuition, what material is the wall or barrier you drew made of? Is it wood? Concrete? Bricks? Specify the material your wall is made of in your drawing. This is extremely important. If you said bricks, draw the individual bricks in the wall.

This wall or barrier represents some form of *limiting belief* in your subconscious mind. It will keep you *stuck* unless you bring the wall down by replacing the limiting belief with a positive one. A limiting belief is any belief that limits your progress. Some of the more common ones include:

- I am not enough.
- I can't afford it.
- I can't do it.
- It just isn't in the cards for me.
- It's too hard.
- I'm not worth it.
- I don't have the resources.
- I'm not good enough.
- Money is the root of all evil.
- I can't be both successful and spiritual.
- No one really wants me...

and so on.

Ask your intuition what limiting belief your wall represents. If, for example, you drew a wall made of bricks, each brick may represent a different limiting belief. Ask your intuition if all the bricks represent multiple layers of the same limiting belief, if each layer of bricks represents a different limiting belief, or if each individual brick represents a separate limiting belief. Label what each brick, row of bricks, or the wall itself represents. This may appear daunting or overwhelming at first, especially if the wall you drew is extremely tall.

Chapter 4: Inspiration Blockers

If your wall is indeed made of bricks, there is a shortcut. Once you remove the bottom layer of bricks, the entire wall will come crashing down. The bottom layer of bricks represents the core limiting beliefs in your subconscious mind. Once these are eradicated, the rest will follow suit.

If, on the other hand, you drew a wall made of a single slab of concrete, it likely represents one major limiting belief.

Intuitively write down the limiting belief(s) your wall represents.

Our beliefs play a major role when it comes to progress or lack thereof. They motivate our actions, and our actions create our results.

Consider that for a moment.

If, for example, your religious beliefs say that certain substances should be avoided, you will be much more motivated to avoid those substances than someone who does not share those beliefs.

Have you ever noticed that those who grow up in extremely wealthy households often become quite wealthy themselves? And not just because they inherit wealth. It's because they are instilled with the belief that success isn't only possible, but expected.

Compare that with those who grow up in very poor or middle-class households, where different beliefs about money and success are taught. They may be taught that money is the root of all evil, or that the only way to earn an honest living is by sweating and grinding, doing hard physical labor for twelve hours a day every day just to scrape by.

I recently worked with a gentleman in his late 30s who had never married but had always wanted to. Unfortunately, he carried the belief he was unworthy of love and no woman would ever want him. Therefore, he didn't do much to seek relationships. The few times he did, he sabotaged them.

The unfortunate truth is most of us go through life acting according to *limiting* beliefs rather than *empowering* beliefs. If you find yourself lacking motivation or *stuck,* you have been acting, at least on a subconscious level, according to a limiting belief.

Read aloud the limiting beliefs you wrote in your success journal. Consider for a moment what these beliefs are costing you. Really dig deep. Are they costing you money? If so, how much money do they cost you per year? Are they costing you relationships? Are they costing you joy and fulfillment?

With that in mind, are you willing and ready to make a change today and choose a new, more empowering set of beliefs? If the answer is "no," do not proceed with the rest of this chapter; it would be a waste of time. Only proceed if the answer is "yes."

Go right now to a place where you can focus completely, without distractions. We are going to go through a process to update your thinking and choose a new belief.

Take a few deep breaths in and allow yourself to clear your mind. Think of an experience that caused you to accept the first limiting belief you wrote down as truth. Trust the first experience that pops into your mind. Go back in time to that experience, but go back to the moment just before it happened. Go back to the seconds immediately before whatever happened that caused you to accept the limiting belief as truth. Take a moment to go there in your mind.

Once there, take a deep breath in... *pause that memory;* *everything freezes...* and breathe out. With that memory on pause, ask someone you love and trust to step into this memory to serve as your advocate and deliver a powerful message that will help you process the memory in a different way, thus forming a new belief.

If you could ask absolutely anyone to serve as your advocate, who would it be?

See that person's greatest and highest self enter into this memory, embrace you, and look you in the eyes. Right now, speak *out loud* (that is extremely important)—as if you were that person's highest self speaking directly to you—the message that person would deliver to help you form a new, more empowering belief. Do that now.

Only continue reading once that is complete.

Great job. And breathe that message in.

Now speak the following words out loud, "I am enough. I am powerful. I am unstoppable. I am capable. I am motivated. I can be, do, or have anything I desire. I've got this!"

Allow yourself to take the message you just spoke and use it to form a new, more empowering belief about yourself. Write your new belief in your success journal and then speak it out loud.

Surrounding yourself with this new belief, hit play on your experience in your mind. How differently do you now process what happened?

In your mind, project this new belief into every part of your life.

In your success journal, answer the following:
- How is your life different with this new belief?
- What are you able to do now that you couldn't do before?
- What actions could you set for yourself now to further reinforce this new belief as truth?

Make a list of action steps that come to you and a commitment to get them done by a specific date and time.

Repeat this process for all limiting beliefs you wrote down.

Once this is completed, ask yourself what happened to the wall that separated you from your desires?

If intuition tells you to repeat this process, repeat this process. If intuition tells you the wall has come crashing down, celebrate! You are that much closer to achieving what you set out to achieve. Place your hand over your heart and declare, "I am amazing!"

With these new, empowering beliefs in place, utilize the following visualization tools to provide further clarity and motivation:

Vision Board

You are a powerful creator. Using a vision board is an effective way to train the part of your brain in charge of creation.

You may have heard about vision boards before; you can find countless videos online of people who have created a vision board and the tools they used to make it more effective. While people have had success with it, many others have not.

This section is intended to clarify the purpose and the "how to" of using a vision board to create success in your own life.

Begin by designating a spot on your bedroom wall that is roughly two feet tall and two feet wide. You may do this with a poster board if you'd like. Divide the space into nine equal sections, making three rows and three columns. Each of these sections will contain goals pertaining to different areas of your life.

Vision Board/Dream Board Map

Wealth	Fame and/or Reputation	Spirituality
Family	Health	Love and Relationships
Learning and Education	Career and Hobbies	Travel and Fulfillment

Chapter 4: Inspiration Blockers

Use the map above to put your goals in their proper places. This is important because each section corresponds with a different area in your brain.

Position your vision board in your room close to your bed. You want this to be one of the first things you see in the morning as you wake up and one of the last things you see at night before you go to bed. Your brain is extremely powerful, and what you put into it as you are going into and coming out of unconsciousness tends to be what you create in your life.

Simplicity is the key. Don't try to be fancy with your vision board. The most effective vision boards are often just a number of statements on post-it notes and simple images printed from Google Images and taped to the wall.

Position your vision board so the middle is about at eye level. If your vision board is too low on your wall, it sends the message that you are "above" going for your goals, so why would your brain try? If it is too high, it tells your brain that your goals are "too far out of reach."

Use a combination of images and statements. Allow some of your goals to be in the form of an image and some to be statements of whatever you desire to achieve. This is important because you have a *left brain* and a *right brain*, and you want to stimulate and train both sides.

Each goal on your vision board should be short-term, meaning the perceived amount of time to achieve it should be no more than six to twelve months. It can be shorter; the main purpose of a vision board is to shorten the amount of time it takes to manifest good things in your life. But please don't put *dream board* or "bucket-list" type goals on your vision board (more about that shortly).

Place only one goal in each of the nine areas of your vision board. You may choose to utilize fewer than all nine areas, but the brain can only focus on so many things at once when it comes to the short-term.

If you are just getting started in the vision board world, make sure to put some extremely small and easy-to-achieve goals on your board. You want to build up as much evidence as possible inside your mind that you are a creator, so consider putting some goals you know you can achieve within a couple of minutes, hours, or days on your vision board so you can prove to your brain that you can achieve them. During the first few months I used a vision board, I put such items as a new belt, which ended up costing me a whopping ten dollars, purchased with the money I earned by picking up an extra shift at my job. I put a picture of an electric hand mixer on my vision board, only to be surprised within a few weeks with a $25 department store gift card, which I used to order an electric hand mixer.

Keep track of all the goals you achieve. Each time you accomplish one of your vision board goals, pull the image or statement off the wall, take a picture of it, and upload it to your social media page in a Vision Board Success Album (more about that on page 77). Then take a picture of you accomplishing whatever it is and upload it to the same social media page. This gives your brain further evidence that you can create good things in your life. It also allows others to get behind you and support you in your goals.

Each morning and evening, stand in front of your vision board. Take a few minutes to look at each goal and visualize having already accomplished it. Activate your feelings. The stronger you can *see* and *feel* each goal in the present moment, the faster it will come into your life.

As you focus on your goals, it is common for fears and doubts to come to your mind. You may hear voices in your head say, "You can't do that!" "That will never happen!" "You aren't able to achieve that!" etc. Keep a pen or pencil in your hand as you look at your goals and write down your fears and doubts. This will get them out of your head so they can no longer do damage. There may be times when you write a single negative thought down and several more come spewing onto the paper. Keep doing this until you feel your "negative thought tank" is completely empty. Do this for all of your goals.

Don't worry, writing these down will *not* reinforce the negative unless you specifically go back and reread the doubts you wrote down (so don't do that!). Destroy the paper once you have finished this exercise.

Writing down your fears and doubts will open up space in your mind to receive action steps to help you get closer to achieving your goals. When these come to mind, immediately write them down—and then go do them. As we discussed earlier in this chapter, your action steps may not always make sense or seem related to achieving your goal, but *do not discard them*.

Note: For additional ideas and vision board strategies, including how to use the following Vision Board/Dream Board Map, please watch my YouTube video titled "How to Create a Vision Board that Works", found at this web address: https://www.youtube.com/watch?v=FipEE992U1g&t=719s.

Vision Board Success Album

This tool is used to reinforce the idea that you are a powerful creator.

Create an album on your social media pages titled "My Vision Board Successes." Every time you get a goal off your vision board, take a picture of the image or statement that was on your wall and upload it to your social media page with the caption "Vision board image: (whatever it is)." Then take a picture of yourself achieving the goal and upload it to the same social media page with the caption "Accomplished (the date)."

Make sure these posts are public and not private. Doing so will serve you in a number of ways:

1) When fears and doubts surface as you go after bigger and bigger goals, you can look through this album and remind yourself how powerful you are at goal achievement.
2) Doing this exercise will help you get past your fears of being seen and judged. A major block many people face is worrying that their peers will think negatively about them if they have success. It is important for successful people to put themselves out there. Some people will like you, and some people may judge, insult, and dislike you. This is part of the journey to success.
3) If you are an aspiring mentor or coach, this tool can help you get more clients. People hire mentors because they see them as authority figures when it comes to achievement. If people don't see you achieving things in your life, you may have a hard time attracting clients. Nearly every time you post a newly achieved goal in this album, someone will ask how you did it. This question is the foundation of creating a successful mentoring business.

Dream Board

What kind of a life do you desire to live? What does your ideal life look like?

A dream board is an important tool because it allows you to visualize how you want your life to be. Its structure is similar to a vision board; it follows the same nine categories illustrated in the map on page 74. While a *vision board* is meant for your next-level goals, your *dream board* is for long-term or bucket list-style goals. While you only want to put one goal in each section on your vision board, you may have as many goals as you like on your dream board.

Place your dream board on your wall to the immediate right of your vision board. Your dream board will give you clarity and direction. It represents your bucket list.

What do you want to achieve in your life? What do you desire to experience? Your dream board will be a visual representation of this. When you look at your dream board immediately before looking at your vision board, the goals on your vision board will have more meaning. They will be stepping stones to achieve everything on your dream board.

Advanced Visualization

In early 2014, I put an image on my vision board that represented a special trip I wanted to take my wife on for our upcoming wedding anniversary. We spent our honeymoon, years earlier, going amusement park hopping in Southern California, and I wanted to re-create it, only this time in a much more lavish way. I priced out the trip to cost about $5,000, which, at the time, was a lot of money for me. I didn't have an extra $5,000 sitting in my bank account and no idea how that money was going to show up.

As I focused on this particular vision board image one day, the idea popped into my mind to look up videos that people posted online from their experiences in these different amusement parks. Many of these videos were made while on the rides, and as I watched them, I felt like I was actually on the rides with them. The more videos I watched, the more I felt like I was there. This created something very powerful within me: a *belief*. A *belief* is a *thought* plus an *emotion*. Watching the videos created a belief in my mind that I was already at the amusement parks. If I had already achieved my goal, it was possible.

I watched videos of the amusement parks in all my spare time for a week.

That weekend, I received a text message from a client who expressed the need to meet with me right away. Sensing the urgency, I invited her to meet me at one of my clinics. She proceeded to tell me that she had suddenly felt strongly prompted to sign up for a coaching program I had just put together that would allow her not only to learn and certify in one of the healthcare techniques I use, but also how to build a practice, increase her income, improve her health and relationships, and ultimately provide the opportunity for her to be hired as a full-time practitioner.

She wrote me a check for $5,000.

I was stunned!

"Did I really create the exact amount of money I needed to fund my trip simply by visualizing it and following the action step to meet with this client when the opportunity presented itself?" I asked myself.

If this only happened once, I could say it was a coincidence. But similar situations have occurred several times since then.

As we've already discussed, our beliefs influence our actions, and our actions create our results. If we desire to change our results, we must first create new beliefs. An effective way to do so is to see yourself in vivid detail having already accomplished the result you desire to create. This can be done using a process known as *advanced visualization*.

Find videos on the internet of whatever you want to accomplish and watch them while imagining yourself in the video. For example, if you want to purchase your dream car, spend time watching videos of people driving your dream car while imagining you are the one driving it. If you want to manifest your dream home, find videos of people doing walk-through tours of homes like the one you desire. First-person point of view is always best. This helps your brain believe that accomplishing your dream is possible. Once your brain believes it is possible, it can generate the action steps necessary to accomplish it.

Remember, what you can *see*, you can *create*. What you can't see, you can't create. When you feel *stuck*, activate the visual part of your brain using the tools in this chapter.

Write the following in your success journal:

"What I can see, I can create. I replace limiting beliefs with empowering beliefs. I stimulate the visual part of my brain with a vision board, dream board, and advanced visualization on a daily basis."

Now place your hand over your heart and declare, "I am amazing!"

"Eric, is there anything that can keep me *stuck,* even with the tools I just learned in this chapter?"

Yes. These are what I refer to as *The Filters…*

Being Stuck Sucks, So Stop It!

CHAPTER 5
THE FILTERS

I'll never forget the Christmas I gave my mom a new water filter. I was nine years old, and I prided myself on giving the absolute best Christmas gifts in the family (or so I thought). I saw a commercial for a water filter and thought it would make the perfect gift for my mom, so I did extra jobs around the house to earn the money to purchase it.

The day arrived to head to the store. I searched through several aisles until I finally found it: the exact water filter I had seen on TV sat pristinely upon the shelf, beckoning me to purchase it.

So I did.

I took it to the front, plopped it down on the counter, and joyfully presented my thirty dollars (which, to a nine-year-old, is like millions!) to the cashier, who smiled as she handed me the receipt. I came home as quickly as I could and, with help from my dad, wrapped this enormous gift to present to my mother on Christmas day. My heart bubbled with anticipation as the days passed and Christmas got closer. Finally, during our traditional Christmas Eve dinner, I could take the anticipation no more, and I insisted she open her present. I smiled from ear to ear as she carefully unfolded each layer of wrapping paper, finally revealing the new water filter.

I watched in awe as tiny water droplets passed through miniature holes in the filter and dripped into the bottom of the container, now clean and purified. The first glass of filtered water blew me away; I had never tasted water so delicious.

It is no secret that we pass us through our own set of "filters" in life. Most of us get caught in traps, while a very small percentage of people reach the levels of success they desire. If so few actually "make it," what happens to everyone else? What stops so many people from living the life of their dreams?

Fear

A number of years ago, my wife and I took a leap of faith and invested in a four-day class to learn to be better presenters and trainers. I'm one of those crazy people who actually enjoys public speaking and being the center of attention, so when I found a class I could attend and learn how to do this properly and get paid for it, I decided to do whatever it took to be there.

The class completely changed our lives. We learned skills we would implement daily as we interacted with prospective clients.

The class instructor asked each of us to commit to at least two dates in the coming month during which we would give public presentations. Being a man of my word, I kept my commitment and held two three-hour classes the following month, both called "Creating a More Abundant 2014", the first class in one city and the second in another.

They were a huge success!

As I followed the template my instructor gave me, attendees hung on my every word as they took copious notes, stood to shout declarations, watched motivational videos, and listened to my story of reaching several inspiring goals.

As the class drew to a close, I planned to introduce a new, full-day class I was developing and offering for an additional fee. My heart pounded as the time to present the proposed class came closer.

Chapter 5: The Filters

"What if I offer this class and no one signs up?" I thought. "How will I feel if I did all this work, and I end up with nothing to show for it?"

Fear darted through my mind. Could my ego stand the blow if no one registered for my next class? Would that mean I wasn't good enough, and that no one liked me?

The temptation to skip the offer was overwhelming. I came extremely close to giving in to the *fear filter*.

How many times have you experienced something similar? How many times have you felt pressed to do something, talk to someone, or make something happen, but didn't because of fear? Perhaps you feared rejection, loss, or failure. How is this showing up in your life? How is it affecting your results? Take a moment and answer these questions in your success journal.

Thankfully, the words of one of my mentors came to my mind that day: "Keep your commitment! People need the message you have to offer!"

I offered the class, finished my presentation...

... and then ran and hid in the other room.

I was terrified no one would sign up, so I didn't want to be in the room to see whether they did. I shut the door behind me, buried my head in my hands, and prayed a single person would value what I did enough to register for my next class.

After several minutes, I finally summoned the courage to peek out the door to see what was going on.

To my surprise, I saw a line of people waiting to register for my next class. I couldn't believe it!

After all was said and done, I asked my wife how we did, and she told me we had made more money in those three hours than we had the entire previous month simply by offering my next-level class. I never would have experienced this great accomplishment had I allowed fear to stop me from keeping my commitment to make the offer.

In your success journal, make a list of all the fears that are keeping you *stuck*.

In order to break free, it is important to understand where fear comes from and why it shows up in our lives.

Fear usually shows up to counter *faith*. Fear is faith's opposite and often comes into play when a person is about to take a leap of faith.

Fear has many definitions, and the one I believe the most accurate is "the anticipation of discomfort." We often get *stuck* and stop ourselves from moving toward a particular goal because we believe we will experience discomfort along the way. This type of fear, though, only exists in the *future*.

I once attended a seminar where the trainer had us all do an exercise I invite you to do as well. "Ready? Raise your hand tomorrow. Come on, go ahead, raise your hand tomorrow.

"Why aren't you doing it?"

It obviously can't be done because *tomorrow* doesn't exist. There is only *today*.

Consider that for a moment. If fear only exists in the future, and the future doesn't exist, what does that say about fear?

"Oh, but Eric, fear is something I *feel*. It isn't logical. Telling me something logical, like 'fear doesn't actually exist in the present,' doesn't help me!"

It's true that most fears are emotional, not logical. If this is the case, what can we do about it?

I mentioned that fear is the anticipation of discomfort, and fears fall into three main categories.

The first is *loss*. Many people get *stuck* when deciding whether to make investments because they fear *losing*. What if they invest time, money, or energy into something, and they don't see an immediate return on their investment?

To combat this type of fear, focus on the *gain*. If you are considering investing in yourself, for example, instead of focusing on what you will put into it, focus on what you hope to get out of it.

In your success journal, make a list of all the changes you feel pressed to make in your life and the changes you commit to making. Then place your hand over your heart and declare, "I am amazing!"

The next type of discomfort people fear is *process discomfort*, or the discomfort of *change*. How many people do you know who want to release weight and get fit but get *stuck* because they think the process of changing their lifestyle, adopting a new diet, and beginning an exercise plan will be too uncomfortable? As Tony Robbins has said, "Change happens when the pain of staying the same is greater than the pain of change." Again, focus on the results you desire. Ask yourself if going through the change is worth it. Most of the time the answer will be, "Yes!"

In your success journal, write down all the ways the changes you are making will be worth it. Then place your hand over your heart and declare, "I am amazing!"

Finally, there is *outcome discomfort*. What if the grass isn't really greener on the other side? What if I quit my job and fail with this new business?

What if, what if, what if... ?

How many people do you know who want to start a business but don't because they fear the outcome won't be what they hope? These people are *stuck*, and the only way to get unstuck is to focus on the *why*, or the purpose for doing whatever it is you want to do. If your *why* is great enough, the *how* takes care of itself.

Let's go back to the emotional aspect of fear. Our emotions are controlled by a certain part of the brain, and our logic comes from another part of the brain. Sometimes simply switching to the logical side of your brain when you feel fear can make a significant difference. When you begin to feel fear, ask yourself, "How much fear do I feel right now on a scale of one to ten?" The act of switching to the logical side of your brain could be enough to dispel the emotion.

But what if this exercise isn't enough? What if the fear keeping you *stuck* is more logical than emotional?

Examples of *logical fear* could be that one will follow in the footsteps of a parent and grandparent who both had a certain bad habit, or that one will inherit a certain condition his or her family has struggled with.

What do you do then?

If this is the case, find the *root fear*.

Read through the list of fears you wrote in your success journal and determine which one you fear the most. Let's say your biggest fear is failure. At the bottom of your list, you would write, "My biggest fear is failure." You would then ask yourself, "The absolutely worst part of failure would be...," and answer the question. Let's say you felt the worst part of failure would be feeling you let your family down. You would say, "The absolutely worst part about feeling like I let my family down would be...," and keep doing this exercise until no more answers come to your mind. The last answer that comes to your mind is the *root fear*.

Take a few moments and do this in your success journal. Find the root of what is keeping you *stuck*.

Once you find it, you can then ask yourself if whatever it is, is actually something to fear. If the answer is no, you've just overcome your logical fear. If the answer is still yes, implement one of the following tools:

Did you ever think there was a monster in your closet or under your bed when you were growing up? Were your parents like most, who just told you that no, there wasn't a monster in your room and therefore you had nothing to be afraid of? Did their response get rid of your fear? If you're like most people, probably not. This is because fear needs to be *validated*, and *action needs to be taken*.

Rather than tell a child there is no monster, have him do something, like grabbing a squirt gun and spraying a few drops of water on the closet door to "melt the monster." Having him *take action* to solve the problem will dispel the fear much more effectively than ignoring it.

The same principle applies to adults.

If fear is keeping you *stuck*, *do* something about it. Take action. Don't allow fear to paralyze you, as so many people do. The more action you take, the less fear will be a factor in your life.

In your success journal, make a list of action steps you feel will help you get unstuck. Set a date by which you will get everything done and firmly commit to doing so. Share your list with someone you love who can serve as an accountability partner. Then place your hand over your heart and declare, "I am amazing!"

Possibly the most powerful tool against fear is *laughter*.

I can still remember a nightmare I had when I was six years old. I was observing a sort of eerie cartoon that took place on top of a tall cliff overlooking the ocean. Sharp, jagged rocks at the bottom meant that anyone who fell off the cliff would die. I watched in horror as the characters in my dream inched closer and closer to the edge. The feeling of helplessness was overwhelming.

The emotions I experienced during this nightmare stayed with me for years. Many times, I lay awake at night, unable to sleep because the images of the nightmare wouldn't go away. I was *stuck*—until I did the following exercise:

I was tossing and turning in bed one evening as the image of the nightmare flooded my mind, when I decided to try something unusual. As the view of the cliff became clearer and clearer, I imagined it had a silly, smiling face that would ask people how their day was going whenever they passed by. Turning the once-frightening image into something humorous was enough to dispel the emotional charge of my fear; I never had the nightmare again. I finally became unstuck.

In your success journal, draw a depiction of your greatest fear. It doesn't have to be a masterpiece; just make some sort of drawing that represents what your fear looks like in your mind. Then add something to the drawing to make it humorous, silly, goofy, or weird.

One client who did this exercise depicted his fear as a giant, squiggly ball of fuzz. When asked how he could turn it into something funny, he shouted, "Oh my goodness! That looks just like my hair in the morning!"

He attached a head and face to the ball of fuzz and began laughing hysterically. This laughter eliminated the emotional charge of his fear. From then on, if he felt this fear creep up on him, he instantly pictured his hair in the morning. Since his hair would never harm him and wasn't at all scary, this fear quickly disappeared. He became unstuck.

Next, picture your fear in your mind. Now imagine yourself growing to one hundred times the size of it. Your fear is now the size of an ant you can easily step on. Your fear doesn't stand a chance against you!

If, after completing this exercise, you still need a little something extra to help you overcome your particular fear, just start laughing. Laugh until you make yourself laugh some more. You may be surprised how laughter can make a difference in your life and in your results.

In any event, you must take significant and immediate action to combat fear. Fear breeds during periods of inactivity. The longer you wait to take action, the more intense your fear will become, and the more *stuck* you will feel. It doesn't matter how many times you tell yourself there is nothing to fear or that your fear isn't real; until you take action, you won't have results. Get moving and decide that fear will no longer be a filter in your life. Then place your hand over your heart and declare, "I am amazing!"

Inconvenience

Imagine you have a relative who lives in Africa. After he passes away, you discover he was extremely rich and left you a check for $10 million, with the stipulation that you fly to Africa and personally pick up the check. There is just one problem: you don't have enough money to purchase a plane ticket. What do you do?

I once posed this very question to my social media feed, and some of the answers I received surprised me.

Some replied, "If I couldn't afford a plane ticket, I wouldn't go." Others said, "I would set the goal of raising the money so I could pay cash for a plane ticket and go pick up the check without guilt." Still others responded, "I would borrow the money and somehow figure out a way to get to Africa as quickly as possible. I would do *whatever it took* to achieve my goal."

Make a list in your success journal of all the reasons you have failed in your life. Seriously. Do it right now. Put this book down and list all the reasons you have failed.

Did you get it done? Do not proceed until you have.

If your list is like that of most people, it likely includes such things as "I didn't have enough money to get started," or "I didn't have the time," or "I didn't have the right schooling."

Each time I teach one of my "Lift Off" seminars, I ask the audience this same question, and I almost always receive answers similar to the three above. These answers all have to do with *resources*, or external factors, when the real problem can be found within the individual—a lack of *resourcefulness*.

Unsuccessful people who find themselves in a situation like going to Africa to pick up a check use a lack of resources (in this case money) as an excuse for not achieving their goal.

Successful people, on the other hand, use their *resourcefulness*, such as tenacity, dedication, determination, and perseverance, to come up with resources when they need them. In this case, they could put the cost of the plane ticket on a credit card. They could borrow the money from a bank or a loved one. They could refinance their car or their house. The point is, successful people do *whatever it takes*, and they do it *no matter what.*

I can't tell you how many people have told me they are *interested* in what I have to say and would love to come to one of my classes to learn more. They tell me how much of a difference it would make to their happiness if their lives were different, and they explain how much they admire people like me for going first and proving it's possible. I graciously thank them for their kind words and ask what they are going to do to facilitate their progress. Sometimes, they look at me funny and tell me they aren't going to do anything different and have no plans to come to any of my seminars. They ask me when I will be coming to their hometown. When I say I have no plans to do so, they act disappointed and say they would come if only the class were a little closer to them. A little inconvenience, this time in the form of travel, was enough to stop them from doing what it took to receive the training they needed to be successful. They remained *stuck*.

There are two types of people in the world: those who are "interested," and those who are *committed*. Those who are "interested" are the dreamers, the ones who say how much they would like a better life. Sometimes they even show up at the seminars but don't apply what they learn. They usually have excuses for why they aren't where they want to be.

Those who are *committed,* on the other hand, learn what they need to do to achieve their desired results, and they make it happen *no matter what.*

The path to success is almost *never* convenient. If it were convenient, there would be no growth; growth only takes place when sacrifices are made.

I once had to make a sixty-hour round-trip journey to get to a training that ultimately helped me achieve the success I have today. Not including the cost of travel, the seminar itself cost me thousands of dollars. But I got there. I proved to myself I would do whatever it took, and my results prove it.

Right now, make a list in your success journal of all the excuses that have kept you *stuck*. You may find this a rather long list, but get it done.

The key to getting unstuck is to turn your *excuses* into *reasons why you will.* For example, the excuse "I'm not going to sign up for that seminar because I don't have the money" turns into "I'm going to sign up for that seminar so I can learn to create more money." "I'm not going to exercise today because I don't have the energy" becomes "I'm going to exercise today so I can have more energy."

Go through your list of excuses and turn each excuse that is keeping you *stuck* into a commitment to take the action that will get you unstuck. Make a solemn commitment to yourself and to others that you will *never* allow these excuses to keep you *stuck* again. Then place your hand over your heart and declare, "I am amazing!"

Money

Let's go back to a few years ago. My wife and I were at a class learning how to be better presenters. On the final day of the class, the instructor told us about a six-month program available to anyone who desired to become the absolute best presenter possible. As I listened to the details of the program, I thought, "This is it! This is the training I've been looking for! I know I can get my family out of the financial pit we are in if I can get this training." I stood up to sign up for the course...

... and then I saw the price. It was $4,900.

We were on welfare at the time. The near-$5,000 price was more than five times what I made in a month at the time, so I started to sit back down. I was very close to getting stuck in the *money filter*.

How many times have you done this? How many times have you felt pressed to invest in some sort of opportunity, but did not because of the price?

Thankfully, my wife grabbed my arm and said, "Get back there and sign up for the program!"

I pointed at the price and violently shook my head. What was my wife thinking? There was no possible way I could come up with $5,000, let alone justify spending that kind of money when we were on financial assistance.

She continued to look at me with those beautiful, loving eyes of hers and asked, "Eric, is it right?"

What could she possibly mean by that? Signing up for the six-month course didn't make any logical sense.

She continued to look at me and asked, "Does it *feel* right to you?"

After a moment to calm my brain enough that I could get in touch with my feelings, I responded, "You know what? I feel peaceful about it."

She looked me right in the eyes and said, "Eric, if it's right, what else matters?"

I went straight to the back table, picked up a registration form, and began to fill it out. I began to hyperventilate and shake because of my fear, but again, my wife asked, "Eric, is it right?"

"Yes," I replied.

"Then what else matters?"

I maxed out every credit card I had, but I signed up for the training.

Chapter 5: The Filters

Realizing I needed to take major action and apply everything I learned to the best of my ability, I went to every training included in the program and tried to absorb everything I possibly could.

Things in my life shifted dramatically.

As I improved as a presenter, my healthcare practice grew. More and more people started registering for classes I was teaching, and within just four months, our income quintupled. I reached a point where I was making more money each month than I had ever made, which was much more than I had invested in the six-month program. I *invested in myself*, and I *received a return*.

The key to overcoming the money filter is to *find ways to invest in yourself.*

Your mind is your greatest asset, and learning just one new skill can make the difference between financial mediocrity and success. Read books, listen to audio trainings, go to seminars, and hire good mentors. Get as much education as you can, and not just the kind that takes place in classrooms. Develop new skills, and use them to create a return on your investment.

Robert Kiyosaki, best-selling author of *Rich Dad, Poor Dad*, is one of my favorite examples of this principle. It has been said that Robert earns $2 million per month in passive income, largely from his real estate investments. He explains that he first learned how to do this by investing, years ago, in a $500 seminar that taught him the fundamentals of real estate. As he registered for the class, he notified one of his colleagues and asked if he would like to register for the class as well.

"Five hundred dollars for a class? That's way too expensive!" was the reply.

Undeterred by his colleague's response, Robert took the class and applied everything he learned, ultimately leading to a massive fortune and the opportunity to teach others how to become wealthy as well. His colleague continued to live the average life he had always lived.

Which cost more in the long run? Investing in a $500 class or *not* investing in the class? Imagine if Robert had fallen victim to the same trap and allowed money to filter his decision to learn how to prosper from real estate. It would have cost him his entire fortune.

How many times has the money filter shown up in your life? How many times have you been presented with an opportunity—maybe a class, a business venture, or simply a purchase that would ultimately lead you to greater fulfillment and enjoyment—but you turned it down because of the money? Remember the difference between those who are "interested" and those who are *committed*. "Interested" people allow things like money to stop them, while *committed* people find a way to make it happen. It all comes down to how much you value yourself and what you desire in life.

Regardless of the price, money can always be found if the value and urgency are high enough. Let me give you an example.

In your success journal, write a description of your dream home. What does it look like? If you're like most people, it's probably a beautiful mansion with plenty of space for you and your family to enjoy all life has to offer.

What would a home like that cost? Depending on the location, probably somewhere in the millions, if not tens of millions.

Now imagine you meet someone who happens to be the owner of the exact home you described. This person is at the age where he would like to retire and move away to a tropical paradise. You find out he has always wanted to give someone an opportunity he never received and will sell his multimillion-dollar estate for just $50,000, as long as the buyer can pay cash up front within the next seven days. You do a walk-through of the house and see that it is in pristine condition. You even have him draw up legal documents, show them to your attorney, and find out that the offer is 100 percent real.

Chapter 5: The Filters

There's just one problem: You don't have $50,000 in your bank account. What would you do?

Just like the scenario with the rich relative in Africa, you would find a way to come up with the $50,000 and move into your dream home. Why? Because you recognize the *value* in it.

The only reason people make a purchase of any kind is because whatever they are purchasing seems to be of more value than the money they are trading for it.

Everyone has access to money. *Everyone*. There are many who choose to limit themselves to what they can see right in front of them (these are typically the ones who use the phrase "I can't afford it…"), but those who achieve success know there is *always* a way to obtain money (or other resources) if an opportunity presents itself.

When a person says, "I can't afford that… ," what he or she is really saying is, "I don't value that enough to trade money for what you are offering."

The problem arises when people don't value themselves, their education, or their results enough to *invest* in themselves.

Constantly seek ways to invest in yourself. Remember the mantra, "If it's right, what else matters?" Trust your heart, and when opportunities present themselves, take immediate action. Attend seminars, read books, hire mentors, and value yourself enough; so when the time comes for others to invest in your products or services, they will feel the personal value emanating from you enough that they purchase your offerings.

An investment in yourself is the greatest investment you can make, and gives you higher returns than any other investment.

A major reason for getting *stuck* is an unwillingness to invest in yourself.

In your success journal, make a list of all the opportunities you felt pressed to invest in, but didn't because of the price. It likely cost you significantly more *not to* invest in those opportunities than it would have to do so.

As I mentioned, within only four months of investing in my first $5,000 program, I quintupled my income. I was making more money than I had ever made before.

And then it plateaued.

I made the exact same amount for three consecutive months. I was extremely grateful for it, but I knew I was capable of more. I had made significant progress with the group mentoring program I participated in. I wondered what I could achieve if I had a personal mentor.

I contacted a professional mentor I respected and asked what she could do for me. She quoted me a price for a certain number of mentoring appointments. I cringed as I heard the number, but the phrase "If it's right, what else matters?" had been engraved in my mind, so I accepted her offer and paid her in full.

Only five days had passed when I received one of the scariest promptings I ever received.

I was on my way to my office when an overwhelming feeling spread over me. It said, "Now that you've hired that mentor, go and hire this other mentor."

Hiring the other mentor cost $25,000.

I sent my mentor a text message to assure her I knew I needed to work with her, but I also felt strongly pressed to work with this other mentor as well. When I asked her what I should do, she told me she would call me later that afternoon.

"Here's the deal, Eric," she said when she called. "This other mentor just announced this morning that he wasn't going to do personal mentoring anymore."

I couldn't believe it. I felt so strongly I needed to work with this other mentor, and now I was told I was too late.

Chapter 5: The Filters

"But," she continued—and in my mind I thought, "Thank heavens for buts!"—"he knows who you are and has actually been wanting to work with you. Therefore, if you can get the tuition in right away, he will make an exception and will mentor you. How soon can you come up with the funds?"

Have you ever had an experience where a word came out of your mouth that didn't come from you? That happened to me that day. As soon as she asked me how soon I could come up with the funds, the word that came out of my mouth was, "Tomorrow."

What!?!?!?

I had never created $25,000 in a single day at that time. I came very close, once again, to getting stuck in the *money filter.*

Thankfully, I simply opened my mind to possibilities, and ideas started coming, including getting a bank loan, applying for additional credit cards, and so forth. I kept thinking, "This is crazy! This is absolutely crazy!"

I took action anyway.

Twenty-four hours later, I called and announced, "I have the $25,000. Count me in!"

In all of several instances I've detailed so far, I *borrowed* money to invest in my education.

"But, Eric, aren't we counseled to avoid debt like the plague?"

There is a major difference between *debt* and *loans*.

Debt is borrowing money for an expense that takes money out of your pocket. Examples include consumer debt, education you don't use, and so forth. Yes, education can fall under the debt category if you don't use it to create a return on your investment.

How many people do you know who spent years in college pursuing a degree they don't use? And now they have thousands of dollars to repay in exchange for their name on a piece of paper hanging on the wall.

A *loan* means using someone else's money to put more money into your pocket. Education you *do* use is a great example. If you go to school to become an attorney, for example, and take that education to create a successful law practice, the money invested in that education would fall into the category of a loan.

For me, hiring personal mentors was a fantastic use of loans. I borrowed tens of thousands of dollars from banks and credit unions to hire the best mentors I could find, then used what they taught me to create an enormous return on investment. While many middle-class people view borrowing money like a crushing weight, the wealthy use loans as a platform to get ahead financially.

Think of it this way: let's say you make $2,000 a month, and what you owe in credit card fees, personal loans, etc., is $10,000. Let's say your expenses are $1,500 per month, leaving you with $500. What most middle-class people tend to do is put the entire $500 toward paying the $10,000 debt. If you paid $500 toward a $10,000 debt, you would need to be paid twenty times to pay the entire amount off, not factoring in any interest.

Now let's say you do what a lot of wealthy, or soon-to-be-wealthy, people do and pay only the minimum payment (let's imagine it is $100) toward your loans each month for a certain period of time, leaving you with $400 to invest each month. Let's say you also take out extra loans to invest in assets, hire a personal mentor to teach you new skills, then start applying these new skills over a twelve-month period. Now, rather than owe $10,000, you owe $50,000, but rather than make only $2,000 a month after applying what you learned from your mentor, you now make $60,000 a month. Let's assume your expenses are now $5,000 per month, leaving you with a monthly cash flow of $55,000. Even though what you owe is now significantly higher, your income is also much higher, and you can pay everything you owe in a single month.

Chapter 5: The Filters

Obviously, this is all hypothetical, but this is how wealthy people think. It is 100 percent okay to borrow money to put toward assets that will help you earn more money, including your greatest asset: your *mind*. If you want to be wealthy, you must act the way wealthy people act. You must get through the money filter.

Doing so will allow you to attract others into your life who are willing to do the same. I often teach aspiring mentors and coaches who want to attract high-paying clients. If they are struggling to do so, it is usually because they haven't become the kind of client they wish to attract.

Consider that for a moment.

If you sell a product or service you are unwilling to invest in, what right do you have to ask others to purchase it from you? If you are an aspiring mentor or coach, and you would like people to pay you $10,000 for mentoring services, if you haven't been willing to pay a mentor or coach $10,000 for his or her services, you probably won't attract people into your life who are willing to. We tend to attract people into our lives who are like ourselves, so it is best to *become* the type of client you wish to attract.

In your success journal, make a list of the ideal client you want to attract. Do they take action quickly? Do they value you and your services and write positive reviews about you? List their characteristics in great detail. Then write out a detailed plan of action to make the necessary changes to become this type of client. Now place your hand over your heart and declare, "I am amazing!"

I will forever be thankful I chose to invest in myself that day years ago. The $25,000 I paid my first major mentor came back several times over.

There is a major difference between *price* and *cost*.

"But, Eric, aren't those the same thing?"

Not even close!

Author Zig Ziglar once told a story about purchasing a bicycle for his son. Rather than pay $65 for a new bicycle, he chose to pay $34 for a used one. He did what many *stuck* people do, which is make a purchase based on *price* instead of *cost*. Within sixty days, the handlebars of the bicycle had to be replaced, which Ziglar did for $5. Three months later, the brakes stopped working, so he paid an additional $15 to replace them. After only six months, the entire bicycle, for which he had paid a total of $54, completely fell apart. Doing the math, he realized he paid approximately $9 per month for his son to ride that bicycle. He then went back to the store and purchased the new bicycle, which his son rode for over ten years. Even though the initial *price* of the new bicycle was higher, the actual *cost,* which turned out to be about 54 cents per month, was much less than that of the used bicycle.

I once did an intuition exercise during which I asked what would have happened had I allowed myself to become *stuck* in the money filter and failed to invest in the original $5,000 program because of the price. The answer came immediately that I would still be on welfare. When I asked why, the response was that doing so would have sent a message to my subconscious mind that I wasn't worth a $5,000 investment; therefore no one else would have valued me either. I have since applied the skills I learned in that $5,000 program to generate millions of dollars. Again, the *price* of the program was $5,000, but the *cost* of *not* investing in the program would have been millions.

Tap into intuition and ask yourself how much *not* investing in the opportunities you listed in your success journal has cost you. Ask for a dollar amount and trust the first number that comes to mind. It is probably much higher than the *price* that you would have paid to invest in those opportunities.

From now on, any time you feel pressed to invest in something, *do it.* It may not make a lot of sense, and it doesn't have to. It didn't "make sense" for me to invest in a $5,000 program when I was still on welfare, but my intuition told me to do it, so I did. Do *not* delay when you feel prompted to act. If you do, you will likely miss out.

It is time to stop getting *stuck* in the money filter.

Write the following commitment in your success journal:

"From this day on, I promise to take immediate action any time I feel pressed to invest in myself!"

Now place your hand over your heart and declare, "I am amazing!"

Embarrassment

I was chosen from among all of the kids in my school district to be a member of an elite singing group during fifth and sixth grade.

This group had it all. We had the flashy costumes, the fancy sound equipment, the bright lights, the dancers, and more. We were known as the best elementary school performing group in all of Southern California. There was a part in the program my sixth-grade year when the music featured a brief saxophone solo. For a bit of comic relief, I was chosen to run out from backstage, dressed as a former U.S. president, with a real saxophone in my mouth, go down on my knees and pretend to play my heart out on that musical instrument. I did this during countless performances and always elicited welcome laughter from the audience.

I then arrived at a performance we learned was to be held outside on a raised cement platform. There were hundreds of people in attendance, and I wanted to show them the very best I had to offer.

I had it all planned out.

After putting on my costume and arming myself with the saxophone, I would burst out from backstage, leap off the cement platform, land on my knees, and create the most magical moment these audience members had ever seen.

And that is exactly what happened...

... with the exception of everything that happened after I burst out from backstage.

As I went to do my leap, I tripped and began rolling, saxophone still in my mouth, down each step of the cement platform until I landed with a giant *thud* at the bottom. A groan of intense pain came screeching out of my mouth. Not only the entire audience but also all seventy-four other student performers in the group burst into a torrent of laughter. After moments of lying helplessly on the ground, I finally summoned the courage to scoop my battered carcass off the pavement and slowly hobble backstage.

While I can easily laugh at the incident now, at the time, it was one of the most embarrassing moments of my life. I considered never singing again. I'm grateful I didn't listen to that tempting inner voice that told me to quit. I continued to sing and perform, which ultimately led to some of the skills I needed to be where I am today.

Embarrassment is an interesting emotion. Any time we feel embarrassed, a chemical is released in the brain that causes a very brief but very real physical sting the body associates with death. We literally feel like we are about to die any time we are embarrassed, which is why we are reluctant to do things that move us outside our comfort zone.

As you progress along the journey to success, you can be sure your embarrassment button is going to be pushed.

Do you remember the story of my first professional presentation and how scared I was that no one would sign up for my next-level class? What worried me most was how embarrassing it would be if no one chose to register. That has actually happened to me on more than one occasion since then. You know what? It was embarrassing, but I didn't let it stop me. I rejected the temptation to curl up in a ball and hide underneath the covers to never be seen again and never feel the sting of embarrassment again.

Chapter 5: The Filters

The key to getting through the *embarrassment filter* is to spend as much time outside your comfort zone as possible. If you strongly fear public speaking and being in front of groups of people, spend time speaking in front of groups of people. If you worry about the embarrassment of rejection, put yourself in situations where you might be rejected. For example, if you are single and afraid of being rejected when asking someone for a date, ask as many people as possible for a date. The purpose of this is to eventually grow your comfort zone to the point where those things are no longer embarrassing.

Keep in mind that things are only embarrassing until they're not. Eventually your comfort zone becomes large enough that things simply don't affect you the way they used to.

Another way people get *stuck* in the embarrassment filter is by comparing themselves to others.

When I was in grade school, just about everyone had a subject they really enjoyed and excelled at. Some were really good at writing. They were the ones who always got A's on anything to do with language arts. Others did really well in science. For some, math was their forte.

On the other hand, most students had a subject they didn't do so well in. Maybe they were really good in math but struggled with science. Perhaps they excelled in sports, but their reading levels weren't the highest. Only a small number of students excelled across the board in every subject they took. Even so, at least a couple of subjects didn't come naturally to them, and they had to work extremely hard to do well.

This is usually the case when it comes to achieving success.

Most people have at least one or two areas of their lives that are going quite well. For example, you may be a person who is spiritual and has fantastic relationships with your family, but maybe your finances aren't where you would like them to be. You could be quite wealthy and feel pretty fulfilled, but maybe your body doesn't look like you feel it should.

Just as nearly everyone has a subject in school he or she does well in, most of us, if we really think about it, have areas of our lives in which we do well. The key is to *recognize* and *celebrate* the successes we have, while gradually and patiently working on the areas we would like to improve.

A mistake people make is to feel jealous and envious of others who excel in the areas they do not, then harshly criticize themselves for not being like the other person. What they don't realize is the other person might be thinking the exact same thing about them.

I once had a mentoring student who, after witnessing how quickly I turned my finances around, sat in my office on the verge of tears because he "wasn't like [me]." I remember sitting in my office, much heavier than I am now, thinking, "Why are you so sad? Yes, I may be slightly ahead of you when it comes to finances, but have you seen your body? You are thin, fit, and in shape. I would trade physiques with you in an instant!" He struggled to recognize and celebrate the areas he *did* excel in. Not only was he extremely fit, he also had a marvelous wife and family and was very active in his faith. Instead, he did what so many of us do, which is focus on what we *don't have* rather than what we *do have*. Doing so kept him *stuck* in the embarrassment filter.

I recently heard a story of a teacher who told his students to prepare for a pop quiz. He passed out the quiz papers with the text face down. When he instructed them to turn their quizzes over, the students were surprised to see nothing but a single black dot in the center of page with instructions to describe what they saw. Once everyone finished the assignment and the teacher had collected their papers, he informed them he wasn't going to grade them on the assignment. He merely wanted to point out that every student had focused on the black dot in the middle of the page. Not one student had mentioned all of the white on the paper. The teacher explained that this is how it is in many people's lives. They spend so much time focusing on the figurative "black dots" in their lives that they fail to recognize the *white* all around them.

In your success journal, answer the following journal prompts:

The black dots I have been focusing on include…

The white parts of my life I now choose to recognize include…

"But, Eric, I literally have *zero* white in my life! The entire page of my life is covered in black dots! There isn't a single area of my life that is good right now!"

If you are one of the extremely few people on this planet for whom this is actually true, I now direct my comments to you. What I'm about to say may not be easy to digest, so I'm going to invite you to continue to read to this only if you are in a high state of teachability.

The reason you are *stuck* is because of your *pride*.

"But, Eric, what about people like those who lived during the Holocaust? Those who were victims of unbelievable hate crimes from people who took everything away from those they victimized. Did those victims get that way because of their pride?"

This is an interesting subject for me because I have relatives who died in Nazi Germany. I have interviewed and studied the lives of several people who survived the Holocaust. Their pride may not have been what caused them to fall into such horrible circumstances, but those who chose to release their resentment and forgive their captors were often the ones who survived.

Those who chose to remain in *victim mode* tended to be the ones who resigned themselves to die. Most of the time, this became a self-fulfilling prophesy. On the other hand, those who lived chose to do whatever it took to survive. Then, once out of the concentration camp, they chose to become healthy and take their lives back.

If you are where you currently are because you have been victimized in some way, decide today to get out of victim mode and take charge of your life.

"But, Eric, that's easy for you to say! I mean look how quick and effortless it was for you to turn your life around."

First of all, it certainly wasn't effortless. I have worked incredibly hard to get to where I am today. Second, even though certain areas of my life did improve quickly, other areas took much longer to improve. All of this happens because of *The Law of Gestation*.

When most people hear the word "gestation," they think of motherhood. For humans to create and birth a new child, the gestation period is approximately nine months. But is this the case in all of the animal kingdom?

No. In fact, every animal has a different gestation period for creating a child. For example, for a mother mouse to gestate a baby mouse, it takes a grand total of nineteen days. It takes a jaguar ninety-three days, or about three months, to gestate a baby jaguar. For an elephant, however, it takes six hundred forty-five days, or nearly two years, to gestate a baby elephant.

If areas of your life simply aren't improving as quickly as you'd like them to, is it possible those areas of your life have different gestation periods?

My money gestation period was extremely fast. I went from welfare to wealthy in less than a year, and I haven't looked back since.

Unfortunately, my fitness gestation period took much longer.

I hired amazing fitness coaches, changed my eating habits, and starting exercising more. Yet the numbers on the scale didn't change like I thought they would. There were times when I threw my hands up in frustration and shouted, "There's no hope for me! I'll *never* get to my ideal weight! Why bother trying?"

Thankfully, I learned a long time ago that *failure* doesn't have to mean *defeat*. When I get knocked down, I choose to get back up and

Chapter 5: The Filters

move forward again. When I learn lessons along the way, I count that as success.

I invite you to do the same.

I once had a mentor draw a large square for me. He then drew lines in the middle of the square from top to bottom and from side to side to separate the square into four smaller squares. To the left of the large square, he wrote, "Learned the lesson," and on top he wrote, "Got the goal."

Create the same diagram in your success journal.

The top left square represents getting the goal *and* learning a lesson. Would you count that as a success? Of course. Who wouldn't?

What if you didn't learn a lesson but you still reached your goal? Would you still count that as a success? Sure! If you reach your goal, of course you're going to count it as a success.

What if you failed to reach your goal but learned a lesson? That question was a bit tougher to answer when my mentor asked me. Of course you want to achieve the goal, but could a life lesson be just as valuable?

Yes, learning a lesson still counts as a success. When my mentor taught me this principle, I realized some truths about my fitness journey. I may not have reached my ideal weight as quickly as I wanted to, but I learned a lot about myself. I was able to heal several emotional wounds. I found and got in touch with my biological family. If it hadn't been for my decision to release weight, I wouldn't have hired a private investigator to find my birth family.

In your success journal, make a list of the successes you have failed to recognize and celebrate.

Celebration is the highest form of gratitude. Whatever you celebrate, you get more of.

Finally, what happens if you don't reach the goal or learn a lesson? This is what we call *going into your story*. Lessons can be learned from every failure, and not recognizing each failure as a stepping stone to success is simply going into a story. So what do you need to do to change your results? Change your story.

I love reading about the Chinese bamboo tree, which is unique. Even though the gardener takes perfect care of it and makes sure it gets plenty of water and sunlight, nothing happens the entire first year after it is planted. Same thing during the second year, and the third and fourth year. Most people would give up after putting in so much time and energy without seeing any visible result. It isn't until the fifth year that the gardener sees a tiny sprout above the ground. Once this happens, in a matter of a few short weeks, the plant skyrockets as much as ninety feet. What took place the first five years after it was planted? It formed its *roots*.

If you want to change your results, just like a tree, start with your *roots*.

Imagine for a moment that your results are like the fruit of a tree. The mistake a lot of people make is to focus only on the fruit itself. Let's say you have an apple tree. Every year, that tree grows hundreds of apples. You enjoy apples, but you decide one year that you're tired of apples and would rather grow oranges instead. You pick all the apples off the tree to make room for oranges to grow in their place. You get so excited for these new oranges to arrive... and to your horror, more apples grow where the old ones were. This happens year after year, and it drives you crazy because you are left wondering why, no matter how many times you get rid of the old fruit, more of the same keeps growing in its place.

How many people do you know get *stuck* in this same predicament in life? They don't like the financial results they are getting, so they switch jobs over and over again—only to find themselves right back in the same financial spot they've always been in. How many people do you know who've tried countless diets, yet they still can't seem to release weight? How about people who have been married time after time, only to realize that, every time they remarry, they find themselves in another abusive relationship? What they don't realize is that simply removing the "fruit" is not enough to create a different result. It is not what is above ground that creates the kind of fruit that grows, it is what is *below* ground. Regardless of how many times I tell an apple tree to grow oranges, unless I dig up the apple tree and plant an orange tree, I will never get anything other than apples.

If you don't like the results you have in certain areas of your life, stop focusing your attention on the results themselves and start changing your *roots,* meaning your *thoughts* and *feelings*. Your thoughts and feelings are what form the "roots" of your "results tree." To change your results, you must first change how you think and how you feel about the things in life you want to change.

For example, if you want to have more money in your life, but you constantly think the way broke people think and have negative feelings about money, you are going to continue to be broke. You must start thinking the way wealthy people think and get yourself to a state of feeling good regarding money. This will lead you to take proper *action,* which will ultimately lead to new *results*.

In other words, your *thoughts* lead to *feelings*, your *feelings* lead to *actions*, and your *actions* lead to *results*. To change your *fruits*, you must change your *roots*, meaning to change your results, you must first change your thoughts and feelings.

In your success journal, write down the following equation:

Thoughts → Feelings → Actions → Results

It wasn't until the beginning of 2019 that I finally saw results in my fitness. I patiently "watered" and "nurtured" the roots of my fitness bamboo plant for five years, and in five months, I released more than sixty-five pounds.

Be patient with yourself. If your gestation period is longer than you would like it to be, remember that you are worth the wait.

Now place your hand over your heart and declare, "I am amazing!"

Judgment

How many times have you been judged or criticized? How many times have you allowed yourself to remain *stuck* and failed to move forward because you were scared of what others might think of you?

Judgment may be the most difficult filter to get through because it requires total and complete self-acceptance, regardless of what others say or think. Judgment can be especially difficult to overcome when it comes from those we love and care about the most.

What can we do when this happens? Do we simply take it, keep our mouths shut, and do whatever is necessary to please the naysayers? Do we allow judgment to stop us in our tracks and keep us from moving forward?

Many do give up. For them, reaching high levels of success and living their dreams simply isn't worth it if they encounter judgment and criticism along the way. Are there ways to deal with judgment and criticism in a positive way so we are no longer affected?

Yes!

The first step in overcoming judgment is to recognize its patterns in your life. As I've looked back on my own life and pondered this subject, I've noticed a recurring set of events that form what I call my *judgment cycle*. It usually begins with learning a skill.

One example was when I learned how to efficiently wait tables and got a job as a server. I am usually a fast learner and have no problem working hard to improve myself, which led to praise and recognition from my supervisors. Their kind words always motivated me to work even harder and become the very best at whatever I was doing. Generally, I eventually reached the top spot. This typically brought out feelings of jealousy from my co-workers, who would then begin to judge, gossip, and spread rumors about me to each other and to my supervisors. I would inevitably lose the approval and recognition I once had from my supervisors, leading me to work even harder and do anything in my power to earn back their approval. This became exhausting, as it seemed my efforts were in vain and nothing I did anymore was ever good enough. I would feel confused, frustrated, hurt, and depressed. Why bother trying if my efforts went unnoticed?

This cycle has repeated itself in various forms throughout my life. In your success journal, write down the steps of the judgment cycle:

1. Learn a skill.
2. Receive praise and recognition from others, often from supervisors, parents, or other leaders.
3. Strive to be the very best.
4. Rouse feelings of jealousy and judgment from associates, leading to backlash and backbiting.
5. Lose praise and recognition.
6. Attempt to earn approval back by working even harder.
7. Fail to earn approval back and feel that no amount of effort is ever good enough.
8. Feel confusion, frustration, hurt, and depression.

Ponder ways the judgment cycle shows up in your own life, and write them down. Your judgment cycle may look different from mine. The important thing at this point is to find where your patterns begin so you can change them from the early stages.

"But why do people judge and criticize in the first place?"

A hotel clerk was once in the middle of a shift when a man trying to check in began to scream at the top of his lungs regarding a problem that was obviously not the clerk's fault. After several minutes, the man finally left, allowing the next customer in line to step forward and check in. The clerk looked up at the new customer with just as big a smile as ever and, joyfully, as if nothing had ever happened, asked how he could best serve him. The new customer, confused, asked the clerk how he could withstand such degrading verbal abuse for so long and not have it affect him.

"It's very simple," was the reply. "I wasn't the actual problem. He wasn't actually mad at me. I just happened to be the one he was taking his frustrations out on."

People have the tendency to see in *others* what they dislike about *themselves*. I call this the *mirror effect*. People love to draw attention away from their own follies and pass along the blame of whatever they are going through to someone else. The flaws they generally point out in other people are typically the flaws they personally struggle with.

Sometimes criticism comes from well-meaning individuals who simply jump to conclusions because they don't have all the facts. I remember the first time I told my family I was going to marry Heather, whom I had only met a few weeks earlier. This was before my family met her, so naturally they responded with skepticism and criticism. Once they met her and saw just how perfect we were for each other, they warmed up to the idea.

Judgment often comes from simple misunderstandings. How many times have you taken someone's intentions to mean one thing when, in reality, they meant something totally different?

Criticism *always* follows those who set out to do good in the world. Think of the greatest men and women ever to walk the earth; they were hated and despised for what they accomplished. Whenever a force for good challenges the forces of evil, forces of evil will do all they can to combat it. Think of Martin Luther King, Jr., who made more progress than possibly any other when it came to helping African-Americans gain civil rights in the United States. He was ridiculed, thrown in jail, and eventually martyred for his cause.

I like the phrase, "Those that let their light shine brightest offend the most cockroaches."

Chapter 5: The Filters

If you are being ridiculed for trying to follow your heart, celebrate it. It likely means you are on to something amazing, and forces of opposition are doing all they can to counter it.

Not everyone is going to like you, and that's okay. Be a force for good in the world, and don't allow negativity to stop you. You are too precious and too valuable.

Write the following commitment in your success journal:

"No matter how many people like me or dislike me, I commit to fulfilling my life's mission!"

Now place your hand over your heart and declare, "I am amazing!"

It is also important to rid yourself of judgment toward others. Any time you judge or criticize someone, you attract that same judgment or criticism into your own life.

A wise man I knew once told me to strive to view other people and circumstances as neither good nor bad, but simply as they "are." For example, if someone cuts you off on the highway, try to view that situation as neither good nor bad; it simply happened.

Does this take some practice? Absolutely. The natural response is to get angry, to want to get even. But does that help? Do increased levels of stress hormones pumping through your body do you any good? Of course not. Remaining neutral and loving regardless of what happens can, however, do amazing things.

Here is an exercise you can do if you truly want to implement this principle in your life. Be warned, though: this tool is only for those who are absolutely committed to creating massive results in their lives and doing everything it takes to get there. If that describes you, grab your success journal and create a list of absolutely everyone you have ever judged or who has judged you. This may be a long list if you're anything like me. As you continue to add names to your list, more and more will come to mind. Do not disregard them when they do. If they come to your mind, it is because they need to be on your list.

Once you feel your list is complete, do an intense emotional clearing technique affectionately named the *Gingerbread Man Exercise*. You will need several pieces of scratch paper and something to write with. Draw a rough outline of a person to represent the first name on your list, including a face at the top. This rough outline may resemble a gingerbread man, hence the name of the exercise. Write the person's name at the top. You now have a visual tool to use.

Go to a place where you can be totally alone and not be disturbed or heard. Your car may be a good place for this, or a secluded field. This exercise has five steps. Step one is to verbally ask the person, by name, for permission to fully express yourself to him or her. You will likely hear a "yes" in your mind. Once you do, proceed to step two, which is to tell that person everything you have ever wanted to say to him or her. If that person judged you, tell him off. Hold nothing back. If you need to throw a tantrum and have a little "come apart," go right ahead. You must get everything off your chest for this exercise to be effective, and you must do this *out loud.* Trying to do this exercise only in your mind will have the opposite effect; it will sink the negative emotions even deeper within you.

Once you have completed the *verbal* release of emotion, proceed to step three: the *physical* release of emotion.

Is there a person in your life you've always wished you could slap or punch in the face? Here's your chance. Take the piece of paper in your hands and physically let all your emotion out. You can slap it, punch it, rip its head off, throw it on the ground and stomp on it, whatever you need to do to release your emotions. This may bring up a lot of tears. If so, wonderful. Let them come. Completely destroy the paper. This can be a cleansing process.

The fourth step is often the most difficult, but also the most important. Pick the paper back up (or the shredded pile of paper, if applicable) and ask for forgiveness for holding those feelings and emotions inside you. Regardless of what that person did to you, *you* must apologize to *him or her* for this exercise to take full effect. The words, "Will you forgive me?" must leave your lips. As they do, you will feel a weight lift off your shoulders.

Finally, imagine that person's greatest and highest self standing before you. Speak as if you were that person's greatest and highest self, who has heard everything you expressed. Speak out loud the words you imagine that person saying to you. These may include words of apology, something to help you understand the circumstances better—whatever comes to your mind. Imagine him or her asking you for forgiveness and you granting it.

While going through your list one by one can be intense and time-consuming, few things are as cleansing and liberating. Go through your list in order, person by person, without skipping anyone. Your subconscious mind put them in the order they are in.

What do you do if, during step one, while asking permission to express yourself, you hear a "no" in your mind?

This is rare, but if it does happen, do *not* proceed. This person's spirit is not ready to hear what you have to say. Rather than express yourself verbally, write this person a letter and then tear it to shreds (do not send the letter).

When you get to the name of a person whom you have judged, use step two to express your remorse for judging him or her. While that person's physical ears won't hear the message, the person's spirit will feel it. You may feel pressed at this point to talk to the person directly. If this happens, make sure you do it. This will be a huge part of your journey to success. Doing this exercise is how we remove our *emotional anchors*.

Have you ever tried to go after a goal but felt as if you were being held down? It was probably because you had some *emotional anchors* keeping you *stuck*.

To recap, go somewhere you can be completely alone and, after creating a visual representation of the person, follow these five steps:

1) Ask permission to express yourself.
2) Release your emotion verbally. Tell the person off.
3) Physically release the emotion. Destroy the paper.
4) Ask the person for forgiveness for holding on to the negative emotion. Ask, "Will you forgive me?"
5) Speak the words you imagine the person's greatest and highest self would say to you.

Do this exercise and rid yourself of the anchors keeping you *stuck*. Then place your hand over your heart and declare, "I am amazing!"

Now that you have removed judgment from your system, allow yourself to be filled with love toward yourself and others. When your entire being is filled with love, there is no room left for judgment.

Love acts like a shield around you, protecting you from the effects of judgment and criticism. See yourself as the amazing person you are and recognize your positive characteristics. A great way to do this is to stand in front of the mirror each morning and tell your body how much you love it. Grab your belly and say how beautiful it is. Rub your hands along your body and give yourself compliments. This not only helps you build confidence, but studies have shown this can actually help your body be healthier and function more efficiently.

What if the judgment comes from those closest to you? What do you do when you have a dream, take steps to pursue that dream, then encounter opposition from members of your own family?

One of my mentoring students encountered this in a fierce way. She had a dream of improving her life. When I first met her, she was bulimic, broke, single, lonely, constantly stressed, and afraid of exploring things beyond the boundaries her parents set for her. When she decided to invest in one of my mentoring programs, she experienced major backlash from her family. They told her how foolish she was for pursuing her dreams and "breaking the mold" her family had set. One of her sisters cut ties with her completely. This broke her heart. She loves her family deeply and struggled with the idea that her choices didn't please them.

How many times have you experienced this? Have all of your loved ones supported every decision you have made? Or have you experienced fierce opposition when you chose to pursue a different path than what was the norm in your family?

When this happens, set clear boundaries. You deserve to be respected and treated with kindness. Don't let anyone, regardless of who he or she is, try to tell you otherwise. It is perfectly okay to limit the amount of time you spend with those who do nothing but bring you down.

You have a mission in life. No one has the right to keep you from fulfilling that mission.

Thankfully, my student followed her heart and continued to push through the rough times. In less than a year, she overcame her eating disorder, started making more than $10,000 per month, and married the man of her dreams.

I once read of a husband who was absolutely fed up with his wife's negativity. He loved her dearly and wanted to preserve the marriage, but her constant belittling and criticizing made keeping their relationship alive extremely difficult. They decided to see a marriage counselor, who suggested that, whenever she fell into a fit of negativity, he politely excuse himself from the room. He would tell her, "I love you. I am leaving the room. I am not leaving the relationship." He set a clear personal boundary that meant he would no longer listen to his wife's negativity. It didn't take long for the problem to be resolved.

In your success journal, write down three personal boundaries you would like others to follow when they are around you. They could include such phrases as "Be respectful when talking to me," "No complaining while around me," "No gossiping around me," or whatever you wish. Once you have these rules set and written down, visualize yourself posting these rules around your personal space, so that all who come in contact with you feel their energy and know to follow them. Now place your hand over your heart and declare, "I am amazing!"

What do you do if the criticism persists?

You can't avoid people completely; you will simply have to deal with them. You can't kick everyone out of your life, especially if it is your spouse or others you live with who are judging you. If you are in this situation, surround yourself, as much as possible, with people who love and support you. You are the average of the five people you spend the most time with, so choose positive people to be your friends who will encourage you to follow your passions and your dreams. The right friends can help you get unstuck.

Finally, realize that you aren't going to please everyone, no matter how hard you try. I like this quote from the book *Light is the New Black* by Rebecca Campbell:

> *You are not for everyone. The world is filled with people who, no matter what you do, will point-blank not like you. But it is also filled with those who will love you fiercely. They are your people. You are not for everyone, and that's OK. Talk to the people who can hear you.*
>
> *Don't waste your precious time and gifts trying to convince them of your value. They won't ever want what you're selling. Don't convince them to walk alongside you. You'll be wasting both your time and theirs and will likely inflict unnecessary wounds, which will take precious time to heal. You are not for them and they are not for you. Politely wave them on and continue along your way. Sharing your path with someone is a sacred gift; don't cheapen this gift by rolling yours in the wrong direction.*

Chapter 5: The Filters

When you encounter judgment, celebrate it. You are probably on the right track and doing some good in the world. Make sure that, deep down, you believe you are enough regardless of what other people say and do. It will be this confidence that helps you get unstuck.

Write the following in your success journal:

"From this moment on, I replace judgment with love. When I encounter judgment from others, I celebrate because I am on the right path."

Now place your hand over your heart and declare, "I am amazing!"

The Jonah Effect

Most of us have a tendency to hide from our own greatness. As crazy as it sounds, more often than not, we run away from, or blatantly reject, things that could potentially enhance our lives, help us be better, or allow us to become unstuck. I can't tell you how many times my wife has come into our bedroom to find me with the covers pulled over my face.

"What are you doing?"

"Shhh... I'm hiding!"

"You're hiding? From what?"

"I know I'm supposed to reach out and connect with so and so, but I'm scared to..." or "I feel pressed to do this, but I don't want to..."

I have noticed this tendency not only in my own life but also in the lives of those I mentor. I've sent text messages to my students asking if they've done their action steps, only to be told they haven't because they are hiding.

This tendency is evident throughout history. Consider the man this concept is named for. In the Bible, Jonah was called by God to prophesy destruction over the people of a city named Nineveh, "for their great wickedness is come up before me," God said. Jonah decided to hide from God; so, instead of heading to Nineveh, he boarded a boat heading in the opposite direction.

En route, a great storm arose that caused huge waves to crash all around the boat and put the lives of all who were aboard in peril. Jonah realized God sent the storm, and that he needed to be cast into the sea to calm the storm. The sailors tossed him into the sea, and he was swallowed by a giant fish, in whose belly he stayed for three days and nights. He was eventually regurgitated onto land and went to Nineveh to complete his mission. This is perhaps the most classic example of someone hiding from his greatness. Jonah was called to be a prophet, a special messenger for God, yet he chose to give in to fear rather than immediately follow through with what he knew he needed to do.

How many times has this same pattern shown up in your life? Maybe you've felt pressed to start a business, perhaps you've felt good about hiring a mentor, maybe you've wanted to ask a certain someone for a date. But you haven't because you've hidden from the task and the possibility of it not turning out the way you would like it to. But is it also possible you could be hiding from achieving the exact result you desire? While that may not seem to make much sense, it is more common than you might expect.

There are two main ways we hide from our greatness: knowingly and unknowingly. Going back to biblical stories, an example of someone who unknowingly hid was David. David is best known for slaying the giant Goliath and later becoming king, but what happened in his earlier years?

Samuel the prophet was commanded by God to go to the home of a man named Jesse because one of his sons would be anointed the next king. When he arrived, Jesse had his seven oldest sons meet the prophet, yet Samuel didn't feel any of them was the right

Chapter 5: The Filters

one. It wasn't until Samuel asked Jesse if he had any other children that Jesse went to get his youngest son David, who was tending the sheep. When David finally came in, Samuel anointed him to become the next king on the spot. David had not known of the greatness within him, so he had not been inside with his brothers when the prophet came to visit. Once he learned his true nature, he knew he could accomplish anything, including later slaying the giant Goliath when no one else thought it was possible.

The other possibility, as we have discussed, is knowing exactly who you are and still choosing to hide. We read in the book of Genesis that Adam, after partaking of the forbidden fruit, heard God's voice in the garden and hid because he was ashamed of being naked, or in other words, exposed before God.

Inadequacy and *shame*, two major parts of the Jonah Effect, keep people *stuck*.

How many times has this happened to you? How many times have you wanted to hide from your Creator in one way or another?

I've considered this concept many times. It never made sense to me until the day I realized exactly who I was. I was contemplating my life and how frustrated I felt for not getting results as quickly as I wanted. I was on the verge of throwing my hands in the air and accepting defeat. That is, until I was given a very powerful revelation of exactly who I am and what I am to accomplish.

I was told via inspiration how many lives I am here to touch for good, the type of responsibilities I'm supposed to hold in my church, the financial level I'm supposed to reach, what sort of body I'm supposed to have, everything I could possibly achieve in this life. And you know what happened? It freaked me out. It terrified me because I realized I spent way too much time hiding from my greatness. Again, this is what we call *knowingly hiding*, or knowing exactly who you truly are and what you are here to achieve, and still choosing to hide.

Is it possible you aren't achieving your highest potential because you don't know who you truly are?

Take a moment to clear your mind and tap deeply into intuition. As you do, ask for an image of who you truly are and what you are here to achieve. This may come to your mind shockingly quickly. Once it does, immediately write it down in your success journal.

Draw an image of what you see in your mind, even if what you see doesn't seem to make sense. I promise it will make sense to you in time. Next to the drawing, write all the characteristics of the image you see. At the top of the page, write "Who I Truly Am".

If you already know who you are and what you are here to do, yet you are still hiding, it's time to stop. My invitation to you is to get as close as you can to your Higher Power and to lean on Him (or Her) for added strength. Perhaps one of the reasons you are hiding is because some things in your life need to be cleaned up. Perhaps, like me, you simply feel overwhelmed with the level of responsibility you know you need to bear. If this is the case, please remember you don't have to achieve everything at once. My mother once called me on the phone, and while we were talking she said, "Eric, you sound absolutely exhausted. What's going on?" I told her everything I was trying to accomplish in my life.

She replied, "That's great, but you don't have to achieve all of that at once. You have an entire lifetime to achieve that."

She was right. I was beating myself up for not accomplishing before I was thirty years old what I was to accomplish over a lifetime.

In your success journal, write about the type of hiding you've been doing. Then create a plan of action to break this habit. Once you have finished, read your plan of action out loud to yourself, then place your hand over your heart and declare, "I am amazing!"

Many who experience the Jonah Effect also experience the *imposter syndrome*, which is feeling like you don't deserve the

Chapter 5: The Filters

success you've had. You believe the good things that have happened to you were a fluke, not that you actually earned or deserved them.

According to author Vanessa Van Edwards, there are five main ways the imposter syndrome shows up in our lives. As you read these five questions, look for ways they could be showing up in your life.

1) Do you ever feel like you don't deserve your achievements?
2) Do you ever secretly worry that people will find out you aren't worthy?
3) Do you dismiss your successes as simply being luck or timing?
4) Do you believe you have tricked others into believing you are more successful than you really are?
5) Do you believe others overvalue your success?

If you answered "yes" to two or more of these questions, you probably have experienced the imposter syndrome in at least one area of your life. This is quite common; seventy percent of people will feel the imposter syndrome at some point in their lives.

How is this showing up in your life? Do you downplay your wins because they don't show up exactly the way you thought they would? Do you fail to celebrate your achievements?

If any of this is true for you, the imposter syndrome could be keeping you extremely *stuck*. Thankfully, there is a way to combat this.

From now on, whenever you hear in your mind that you aren't good enough, that you are a fraud or anything of the sort, recognize that this is simply part of the imposter syndrome and doesn't actually come from you. Whenever this happens, get a piece of paper and write down the negative chatter that comes to mind.

"But, Eric, what if the negative talk is coming from other people?"

As we discussed in the previous chapter, the more good you do in life, the more opposition will try to stop you by influencing others to say mean things about you. People usually do this because they are jealous or simply don't understand you. They might start rumors, gossip, or blatantly lie about you.

I experienced this during my ultimate test, which you'll read about in Chapter 9.

If you are going through this, please know the comments you hear from others have a lot more to do with them than with you. Hold a space of love for those who oppose you and, if and when appropriate, ask yourself if there is any truth to what they are saying. Ask yourself what lessons you can learn from the situation, then implement these lessons. We will discuss this more in Chapter 9.

Utilizing your vision board success album is another way to combat the imposter syndrome.

"But, Eric, isn't that bragging?"

Nope.

A brag is only a brag when you are comparing yourself to someone else and putting the other person down. There is nothing wrong with posting about your own successes. I'm not saying to do so in a way that draws a lot of attention to yourself. But having an album of pictures of your accomplishments on your social media page both gives your brain evidence you can create amazing things in your life and allows others to get behind you and support you. When the imposter syndrome rears its ugly head, look at these pictures and reach out to your *cheerleader friends,* those always willing to lift you up. Ask them to write good things about you that you can read any time you feel the imposter syndrome.

Take a moment right now to post something good about yourself on your social media page. Then place your hand over your heart and declare, "I am amazing!"

If you really want to take this tool to a new level, stand directly in front of someone so you are both facing each other. Invite that individual to look directly in your eyes and, for sixty seconds, answer the question, "The greatness I see in you is..."

Once sixty seconds have passed, return the favor. Be a good receiver. Don't discount what your partner sees in you. This can be critical in helping you overcome the imposter syndrome.

Go right now, get a partner and do "The greatness I see in you" exercise. Then place your hand over your heart and declare, "I am amazing!"

How did you do with that exercise? Was it easy for you to receive the good things your partner said? Or did you feel inclined to disregard them?

Another tendency of the Jonah Effect is to dismiss compliments. How many times have you given someone a compliment only to have that person deflect it? How many times have you found yourself doing this?

Is it difficult for you to receive positive words of affirmation? Do you believe you'll get a big head if you receive them graciously?

People often hide from compliments because they fear they will become egotistical if they accept them or they fear living up to their portrayal in the compliment. While many of us fear failure, an even greater percentage fear success.

Why is that? Some believe success will change them. Do you know people who believe that lots of money would make them greedy, prideful, or sinful in some way?

Money doesn't change anyone. It simply makes you more of who you truly are inside. The same is true with compliments; they bring out the greatness you already have inside you. From now on, when someone gives you a sincere compliment, simply say, "Thank you." Don't dismiss the compliment or deflect it back on the other person.

This same concept applies to compliments you give yourself.

How much love do you give yourself each day? If you're anything like me, not nearly enough. When was the last time you told yourself you love yourself—or even like yourself? That may seem hokey at first, but it is a powerful way to build confidence and overcome the

Jonah Effect. The higher you raise your personal value, the easier it is to overcome fears, reject the tendency to hide, and step into the greatness you have within you.

Every day, declare, "I like myself. I like myself. I like myself. I love myself. I love myself. I love myself. I unconditionally love and accept myself. I unconditionally love and accept myself. I unconditionally love and accept myself."

If you 100 percent love and accept yourself regardless of your flaws, what need do you have to hide from the world?

A lot of us hide from judgment we perceive will come from others simply because we aren't perfect. This was a *major* limiting belief I had to overcome. When I first decided to accept the role of mentor and trainer, I thought I had to be perfect, or at least *perceived* as perfect, for people to want to work with me. It caused a great deal of disconnect between my students and me. Many said they felt I was inauthentic. This bothered me because, for a long time, I couldn't figure out what they meant. I had the results I said I had, and I really had helped others achieve massive growth in their lives, so why were people saying I was inauthentic?

It was simple: I didn't want anyone to know I had bad days just like anyone else, so I hid behind a mask of perfection and didn't allow people to truly connect with me on a personal level. I worried that, if they knew about all the struggles and imperfections I dealt with each day, they wouldn't want to work with me anymore.

One of my mentors noticed this in me and called me out. He looked me right in the eyes, and said, "Eric, it's time for you to finally step into authenticity." He asked me, "What is it you are so adamantly hiding from?"

I emotionally replied, "All my life, I've been the subject of major criticism. There was never any middle ground; people either loved me or hated me and said really mean things about me. I am worried

Chapter 5: The Filters

that, deep down, all the mean things people have said about me are true; that I really am the horrible person so many people make me out to be."

He invited me into his basement where there was a stage.

"Get up on the stage."

I did.

"Now take off your shirt."

Huh?

"You've gotta be kidding me," I thought. My body and the fact I had a gut were things I had tried to hide for years, and now my mentor was telling me to stand on the stage without my shirt, completely "exposed"?

He continued, "I want you to imagine that everyone you fear is judging you is sitting here in the audience with us today. You are an amazing presenter. You are going to give a presentation to everyone regarding all the imperfections you are worried people will judge you for. Once you've owned each of your imperfections, you can stop hiding from them and finally step into your power."

So I did.

I spoke about how I felt like an imposter and have horrible days just like everyone else. I said I sometimes felt like a fraud, and I certainly didn't have everything figured out like I hoped I would by that point.

It was one of the most uncomfortable things I have ever done. It was also one of the most freeing things I have ever done.

People don't want to think you are perfect. Your imperfections are what make you relatable. Rather than hide from your imperfections, embrace them.

In your success journal, create a list of everything you are hiding from the world. Go through your list, one by one, and own each one of your imperfections by stating, "Even though I (fill in the blank with the imperfection), I still unconditionally love and accept myself!" Do this three times, then place your hand over your heart and declare, "I am amazing!"

It is also time to stop hiding from your problems. Doing so will not make your problems go away. A major difference between successful people and unsuccessful people isn't that unsuccessful people have problems and successful people don't. Successful people face their problems head on and grow themselves to be greater than any problem.

Author Jim Rohn used to say, "Don't wish it was easier, wish you were better." The more you grow, the more you can face and overcome any problem or action step you receive.

Just like Jonah, sometimes you may feel pressed to do something that seems scary and way outside your comfort zone. You may procrastinate fulfilling that action. When this happens, some sort of plateau is usually the result. This happened to me at a certain point in my career. I had been growing by leaps and bounds, breaking records in my business every month. Then, seemingly overnight, it seemed as though someone stepped on the fire hose of my success. My clients started dropping out of their mentoring programs, potential clients started missing their appointments with me, and I nearly lost everything. I couldn't understand what was happening. I was doing so well, only to have everything nearly come crashing down.

It finally dawned on me; I felt pressed for months to complete a couple of action steps, and I ignored them. The two action steps were to release weight and write my first book.

Are you hitting a plateau in any area of your life? Are there action steps you have felt pressed to take but, like Jonah, you've hidden from them because you don't want to complete them? Just like Jonah, is there a message inside you that needs to be shared? The universe may be denying you any more success until you complete the action steps you have procrastinated.

Make a list in your success journal of everything you have procrastinated. Now create a plan of action to get them all done.

It is time to stop hiding. It is time to let your light shine before the world. It is time to truly step into your greatness. Now place your hand over your heart and declare, "I am amazing!"

"Eric, are there people who *never* get caught in these five filters? If so, how can I be more like them?"

Yes. The filters have no effect on certain people. Those people are *children*…

Being Stuck Sucks, So Stop It!

CHAPTER 6
LIKE A CHILD

I will never forget the day I became a father.

My wife was only thirty-five weeks pregnant when she woke up with intense pain and felt she had to get checked out by her midwife.

She never expected to find out she was in labor.

Our beautiful daughter, Ashley, came into this world on April 29, 2012. She was a tiny three pounds fifteen ounces and was rushed to the emergency room because she was so premature. My wife didn't even get to hold our new daughter until the following afternoon.

Thankfully, a very skilled team of nurses, midwives, and doctors expertly cared for our daughter and saved her life.

She spent two weeks in the newborn intensive care unit. My wife and I spent as much time as possible by her side, admiring her, and sending her as much love and positive energy as we could. As she has grown into a beautiful little girl, and as we have welcomed other children into our family, my wife and I have had the privilege of observing the things she and her siblings do.

We read in spiritual text that we are to become "like a child" in all that we do. I've pondered this several times to figure out what this means. Does this mean being immature and childish? Does this mean only speaking in coos and grunts? Probably not.

On my path getting to where I am today, I have learned eight major lessons children can teach to help us get unstuck.

Lesson #1: Children celebrate everything

When my daughter was one year old, she celebrated absolutely *everything* that came into her life. When we gave her cereal to snack on in the car, she would yell, "Yaaaay, cereal!" When we pulled into our driveway, she would recognize where we were and shout, "Yaaaaay, home!!"

As children grow older, these moments of celebration turn into "wahoo," then to high fives. Over time, however, as children become adults, they stop celebrating victories altogether. As we become adults, we somehow feel it isn't appropriate to be happy when little victories come our way.

As discussed in Chapter 5, celebration is the highest, most sincere form of gratitude. When we celebrate something, we literally give thanks for it.

Consider how this applies to children. Are you more likely to give a child more of something when he or she throws a tantrum over not having it? Or do you feel more inclined to reward children if they are grateful and appreciative?

As adults, when there is something in our lives we desire to have, we mistakenly focus on the fact that we *don't* have it.

A major example of this is money.

How many adults do you know who have thrown a fit over not having enough money? This is why celebrating is so important.

T. Harv Eker, author of *Secrets of the Millionaire Mind*, counsels us to celebrate even finding a penny on the ground because you are sending the vibration of gratitude into the universe, so you can receive much more of whatever it is you're celebrating—in this case, money.

"So, Eric, does that mean we have to throw a huge party every day to commemorate every tiny thing we do right?"

No. What I am saying is to show *gratitude* for everything good in your life.

The Hawaiian Huna philosophy says, "Bless that which you want." Live life as if you were already experiencing what you desire, and then watch how fast what you desire comes into your life.

Write the following in your success journal:

"From now on, I choose to celebrate all good things in my life."

Now place your hand over your heart and declare, "I am amazing!"

Lesson #2: Children are quick to forgive

How long does a child hold a grudge? Most of the time, not very long. What do they do if someone upsets them? They throw a tantrum, release their anger, and go on playing as if nothing had happened.

What would your life be like if you released negative emotion as quickly as children?

Even as adults, it is important to release emotion. There are times when I'm with a mentoring student and see from her body language that she has a lot of pent-up emotion holding her back from achieving the greatness I know is within her. I send her to a place where she can be totally alone to throw a tantrum. Clients look at me as if to say, "Wait a second, I can't do that! I'm a grown-up! Grown-ups don't throw tantrums!"

Many adults mistakenly think they have to hold their emotions in.

Were you told not to cry as a child? Perhaps you got in trouble if you cried or threw a tantrum. That carried over into your adult life, making it difficult for you to release pent-up emotion. Allow yourself to throw a tantrum every now and again. Make sure no one is around who can hear or disturb you; go somewhere you can be totally alone and express yourself completely. Allow yourself to feel and release all that needs to be felt and released.

I tell people, "If you're having a crummy day, allow yourself to recognize and validate the fact that you're having a crummy day." Tony Robbins counsels, "See it as it is, but don't see it worse than it is." Once you've acknowledged you're going through a rough time, throw your tantrum, get the emotion out, then pick yourself up and move on.

Write the following in your success journal:

"I choose to forgive quickly and release negative emotion easily."

Now place your hand over your heart and declare, "I am amazing!"

Lesson #3: Children allow themselves to laugh and be silly

Some of the funniest things I ever heard have come from my daughter's mouth. I'll never forget the time when, from across the house, I heard, "Oh, that was a *big* fart! But where's the little fart? Oh, there it is, I found it!"

How many times have you seen a child on a playground invite his or her mom or dad to join in the fun only to be turned down because the mom or dad doesn't think it would be appropriate to play the way the child is playing?

What would you like to do if you knew no one was looking? How silly does your inner child yearn to act? Unfortunately, you don't allow yourself to tap into your inner child because someone once stuck a finger in your face and told you to grow up.

Complete the following sentence in your success journal:

Chapter 6: Like a Child

"I don't feel I can be completely childlike because…"

You may be surprised what comes to your mind as you do this exercise. Once you do, create a plan of action for overcoming this limiting belief.

We have discussed the importance of releasing emotion, and laughter and silliness are the fastest, most effective ways to do so. The next time you are upset, do something totally and completely silly. Doing so disrupts the signals being fired from your brain telling your body to be upset, and pretty soon you're not upset anymore.

My wife demonstrated this principle beautifully one evening when I came home grumpy from work. I stormed into our bedroom and began to blame her for all of our problems. I puked and spewed negativity, and demanded that my wife change.

She patiently listened to my ranting and finally responded, "Yes, Eric, I could do that… Or I could make you look like a carrot."

Huh?

I was wearing a bright orange polo and happened to be standing in front of a green towel that was hung up to dry. My wife grabbed the towel, wrapped it around my head, pulled my orange shirt up just under the towel, and gleefully announced, "You're a carrot!!"

My brain had no way to compute this odd behavior.

It caused a *pattern interrupt*. My brain stopped firing angry signals, and I began to laugh. I laughed so hard I could no longer remember what I had been angry about.

Give this a try. The next time you feel absolutely furious about something, do something off-the-wall silly, and watch how quickly your anger dissipates. Silliness is a great way to get unstuck.

Write the following in your success journal:

"I allow myself to be silly and childlike."

Now place your hand over your heart and declare, "I am amazing!"

Lesson #4: Children are dreamers

Did you play pretend when you were younger? Of course you did. All children do. They have no problem creating things in their mind because, to them, there are no limitations, and everything is possible. It is only when we grow older that people tell us to be "realistic," and we stop dreaming big.

Answer the following questions in your success journal:
- What would you do if your life had no limits?
- What would you do if everything you dreamed about became reality?
- What would you want to do?
- What experiences would you want to create?

One of the first mentoring principles I like to teach is called the *ABCs of Success*. Draw a dot in your success journal and label it "A." Then draw another dot up and to the right of the first dot. Label it "B". Do this one more time so you have three dots leading upward and to the right. Label this third dot "C."

Your "A" dot represents where you currently *are* in life.

Your "B" dot represents your next-level goal in each of the five F's of success (Faith, Family, Fitness, Finances, Fulfillment), meaning where you hope to *be* in the next six to twelve months. This also represents your *what*, meaning what you will focus your attention on next when it comes to personal improvement. For example, if your current financial situation is you are now making $5,000 per month, your next-level goal might be to make $7,500 or $10,000 per month. As we discussed in Chapter 4, these are the goals that go on your *vision board*; goals that should take no more than six to twelve months to achieve. If you have items on your vision board you know will likely take more than twelve months to achieve, you may want to replace them with more incremental goals.

Your "C" dot represents where you *see* yourself long-term. Using money as an example again, if your "A" is $5,000 per month, and your "B" is $10,000 per month, your "C" might be enjoying life as a multimillionaire. This is what your *dream board* is for. There are many who confuse a vision board with a dream board or think they are synonymous; when in reality, they are two very different and very important tools. Using one without the other could cost you. While your vision board is filled with "B" goals, your dream board is where you put your "C," or bucket list, goals. There is no limit to how many images you put on your dream board because this represents everything you hope to achieve and experience before your life is done. Your dream board represents your *why;* it gives purpose and clarity to your vision board's focus. With a dream board on the wall, you can always make sure your vision board goals are in line with your overall mission and purpose. I look at my dream board multiple times a day to remind myself why I do the things I do.

Write the following in your success journal:

"I allow myself to dream big."

Now place your hand over your heart and declare, "I am amazing!"

Lesson #5: Children don't hesitate to go after what they desire

My son, Bradley, is at the age where he loves to grab things. When he sees something he thinks would be fun to play with, he doesn't hesitate. He just reaches out and grabs it.

Adults? Not so much.

We adults often see things we desire, but we hesitate. We believe we have to "think about things," and therefore miss out on critical opportunities. As we discussed in Chapter 4, "thinking about things" keeps you extremely *stuck.*

How many people do you know who would love to quit their job and start a business? They almost always have a "logical" answer why they don't, which usually has to do with fear.

Children? They see something they want, and they go for it.

Have you ever seen children do something, and when you ask why they did it, they respond with, "I don't know"? The truth is, they don't know why they did what they did. They don't make decisions based on logic, fear, or consequences. They simply act on intuition.

If you want to get unstuck and improve your results, it is important to act based on *intuition* and your *feelings* rather than logic. Get out of your head and into your heart. Whenever you feel *stuck*, lightly tap your heart. This will open your heart chakra and allow you make decisions from a space of feeling and intuition rather than logic. The pathway to success is often extremely illogical.

Write the following in your success journal:

"I listen to intuition and take immediate appropriate action."

Now place your hand over your heart and declare, "I am amazing!"

Lesson #6: Children don't give up

Have you ever observed children learning to walk? Do they make mistakes, stumble, fall, and sometimes hurt themselves? Absolutely. But do they let that stop them? Absolutely not.

How many times have you given up on something you really wanted to accomplish simply because you failed the first time?

Failure is part of success. The only way to become *perfect* is to first be *imperfect* and learn from your mistakes. Just as you would never scold a child learning to walk for falling down the first time he or she tries, it is important to allow yourself room to grow, make mistakes, get back up, and try again until you master whatever it is you desire.

Chapter 6: Like a Child

Write the following in your success journal:
"I never give up!"
Now place your hand over your heart and declare, "I am amazing!"

Lesson #7: Children accept help from others

I'll never forget an experience I had during a class my wife and I attended. The instructor told us to get into groups of ten to perform a trust-building exercise. Each of us would have a turn being cradled, meaning the other nine members of our group would stand behind us and form two lines of people facing each other with their arms criss-crossed in such a way that a person could lie down across their arms with their entire body weight supported.

It was one of the most surreal experiences of my life.

I was completely vulnerable. I had to trust my group to support me and not let me fall.

One of the most important principles of success is to always have a mentor. Unsuccessful people try to figure everything out themselves. They don't see the value in having a mentor, someone who can show them how to accomplish the things they want to accomplish much faster than trying to do it on their own.

Playwright Ben Johnson said, "He that is taught only by himself has a fool for a master."

Reaching out for help and guidance is *not* a sign of weakness. Have you ever seen an Olympic athlete without a coach? Absolutely not. They are the best in the world at what they do, yet they still hire coaches as an extra set of eyes so they can continue to improve and be the absolute best they can be.

If you want to get unstuck, get a mentor. Find someone who has what you want in life and pay whatever is necessary to hire that person.

Write the following in your success journal:

"I accept help from others and always have a mentor."

Now place your hand over your heart and declare, "I am amazing!"

Lesson #8: Children are teachable

A huge indication of how successful a person will be can be measured by what is called his or her *Teachability Index*. This measures your *willingness to learn* and your *willingness to change*. Both are equally important.

You've heard that children are like sponges; they soak up as much knowledge as they can, and are constantly learning and growing. You should never stop learning, growing, and changing. The most successful people in the world recognize the fact that they don't know everything and constantly learn more to improve. Go to seminars, read books, listen to motivational audios, and work with qualified mentors and coaches. Become a student throughout life and watch your results continue to increase.

Write the following in your success journal:

"I am always willing to learn and always willing to change!"

Now place your hand over your heart and declare, "I am amazing!"

"Eric, how can I truly become more childlike? I just have too many responsibilities to really let loose and find balance."

Balance is achieved by implementing *blue screen time.*

CHAPTER 7
BLUE SCREEN TIME

Many people follow the mantra "all work and no play." The extreme go-getters work hard every day because, to them, there simply isn't time for anything else. We often see this tendency with full-time mothers. Full-time mothers are so selfless, and they love their families so much, they rarely allow time just for themselves.

"But, Eric, there is just so much to get done," they say to justify themselves. "I simply don't have time for myself!"

Unfortunately, many people think this way. They are always on the go and never allow any down time. As counterintuitive as it may sound, this is a great way to remain *stuck*.

I am going to suggest that you allow yourself some time each day to pamper yourself, rest, and recuperate.

Consider that for a moment. If you were trying to strengthen your muscles, what would you do? You would likely spend time lifting weights on a regular basis. Those who do so know not to exercise the same muscle group every day until they pass out from exhaustion. They know they need to do a certain number of repetitions, rest, perform a certain number of additional repetitions, then rest again. They give their body a certain number of days to rest completely so their muscles can heal and rebuild stronger than they were before.

The same concept also applies to the brain.

If you want your brain to continue to grow stronger and help you produce greater results, you must allow it some down time, or what I like to call *blue screen time.* You know how a computer screen will go completely blue when recharging and updating itself? It's the same idea.

Each person is different; everyone has different ways to relax and recharge. For example, my wife takes care of our young children each day as a stay-at-home mom, but she takes a warm bath by herself each night to recharge and let her body and mind relax. This is her way of getting blue screen time.

What do you enjoy doing?

In your success journal, make a list of activities that recharge and rejuvenate you. The purpose of this chapter is to convince you to set aside an hour every day to do at least one of the activities you just wrote down.

Let me explain what I mean.

Imagine you work a regular nine-to-five job, and your supervisor lets you know he has a new idea you are absolutely going to love. Instead of working eight hours each day, you will work sixteen hours each day, and you won't receive any increase in salary. Isn't that a wonderful idea?

If you are even remotely sane, you think an offer like that is ridiculous. Who in his right mind would be okay with doing twice the work without receiving twice the pay?

Just as it is important to compensate company employees for the work they do, your brain needs to be compensated for the job it does and rewarded for going above and beyond. Just like a company employee won't stick around if he isn't properly compensated for doing an excellent job, your brain will eventually stop producing results if you fail to take time to compensate it. This is another way many people get *stuck.*

Chapter 7: Blue Screen Time

How do you compensate your brain? Through *play*, *celebration*, and *relaxation*.

What do you do to recharge? For my wife, it's taking a warm bath each evening. For some, it might be dining out at a nice restaurant. For others it may be taking walks in nature. For extroverts, it might be spending time with friends and going to social gatherings. For introverts, it likely consists of being alone and doing some quiet activity, like reading a book, playing a favorite musical instrument, or watching favorite television shows.

"So, Eric, are you encouraging people to spend long hours each day just 'vegging' in front of the television?"

No, but that wouldn't necessarily be a bad thing every now and then. Again, each person is different, and each person needs a different amount of blue screen time each day. Some people do well with just a few minutes. Others, including myself, often need a couple of hours each day to recharge.

One of my favorite things about owning my own company and setting my own schedule is that I get to decide how late I sleep each day. I usually don't start my workday until early afternoon so I can fully honor my natural sleep schedule as a night owl.

Some might argue against doing so, saying it's important to wake up early each day, even before the sun comes up, jump immediately out of bed, and start working the moment your feet hit the ground. While this certainly works for some, it isn't right for everyone. My invitation to you is to find what honors you and your personality the most, then make it a priority to do whatever that may be as often as you feel you need it. And yes, if that includes watching a few minutes of uplifting television, go for it. Again, I am not encouraging you to go overboard and use this as an excuse to be lazy and fail to do the things you need to do. Simply figure out what helps create balance in your life, and make that a priority.

And yes, this includes stay-at-home mothers who think they never have enough time for themselves.

What *do* you have time for?

We all have the same amount of time: twenty-four hours each day. It is what we do with that time that matters. We generally make time for all our *musts*. For example, we *must* eat to stay alive. If we have a regular job, we *must* go to work on time to stay employed. If we ever have a major emergency, regardless of how busy our lives are, we find the time to address it because it suddenly became a *must*. We always have time for our *musts*, but not so much time for our *shoulds*.

How many *shoulds* do you have in your life?

"I *should* go to the gym and exercise."

"I *should* go out and mow the lawn."

Remember, doing things because you *should* can keep you *stuck* because it means acting at a social level of motivation.

The key to blue screen time is making it a *must* in your life because, without it, you're eventually going to hit a plateau and feel *stuck*.

If you've hit a plateau somewhere in your life, it may be because you aren't taking good enough care of yourself and rewarding yourself from time to time. So your brain rebels and says, "I'm not going to produce any more results until I start getting some appreciation around here!" When that happens, you better do something quick to show your brain how much you love it. There's a reason my wife and I go on vacation roughly every twelve weeks. We understand this concept, and we allow ourselves plenty of time to recharge.

In your success journal, make a commitment. Decide how much blue screen time you will give yourself each day and what you will do during that time. Then make sure you do it.

Along with the need to recharge, each person has a number of basic needs. Tony Robbins calls these *the six core human needs*.

Chapter 7: Blue Screen Time

#1: Certainty

Part of us craves certainty and security in our lives. Most people want to be in a committed, loving, long-term relationship because they want to be certain they will always have a significant other and all the benefits that brings. Unfortunately, a lot of people take this to the extreme and stick with things that don't serve them, such as abusive relationships or mundane jobs, simply because they fear uncertainty and the unknown.

Have you ever rented a movie you already saw, ordered the same dish multiple times at a particular restaurant, or visited an amusement park and ridden the same rides you had been on before? You did so because you already knew you would enjoy those things, so you chose to repeat them rather than risk doing something different you might not enjoy as much. This helped fill your need for certainty.

#2: Variety

In contrast to need number one, we also have a need for variety. Most people are certain they would enjoy a delicious steak dinner, but can you imagine if you ate that exact same meal every evening for the rest of your life? After only a couple of nights, you would start to strongly dislike steak because it no longer filled your need for variety.

#3 Significance

Each of us craves significance. For many women, this comes in the form of their desire to be mothers. They understand that raising a new generation of people and teaching them positive things so they will have wonderful, meaningful lives is significant. Some people dream about inventing something that would end world hunger and bring about world peace because doing so would fill a need for significance in a major way. Many people become mentors and coaches because they hope to feel significant by changing the lives of others.

#4: Love and connection

Even the most shy, introverted people want to feel loved and able to connect with others. Deep down, nearly everyone enjoys a good handshake, a warm embrace, or cuddling with a significant other.

#5: Growth

"When you stop growing you start dying," according to American writer William S. Burroughs. T. Harv Eker says that true happiness comes only from progress. Consider that for a moment. If you aren't doing something meaningful in your life and constantly challenging yourself to be better, you are missing out on a fundamental need. Continue to set goals, read books, go to seminars, and work with excellent mentors. Does this mean never be grateful for what you currently have? Of course not. There is a major difference between gratitude and complacency. Strive for constant growth in every area of your life.

#6: Contribution

We are all part of a human family, and we all have the ability to contribute to something bigger than ourselves. For some, that may mean missionary service in foreign countries. For others, it may mean becoming a doctor to save lives. It could mean creating a life-changing product or service and starting a business to get it in the hands of as many people as possible.

"That's all nice, Eric, but what does this have to do with blue screen time?"

There are five main levels of brain activity. Each level fills at least one of the six basic needs.

Level One Brain Activity: Full-On Blue Screen Time

This is the least of the five brain activity levels. It usually occurs at night as one is unwinding to go to bed or after prolonged intervals in Level Five, which will be explained momentarily. When I am in Level One, I have to be by myself doing absolutely nothing that requires me to think. I usually close my eyes, listen to meditation music, take a nap, or watch fun videos on YouTube. I often watch videos I've seen before or read books I've read before, which helps fill the need for certainty at this lower level of brain activity.

Level Two Brain Activity: Passive Learning

While this is still a level of relaxation and recharging, those in Level Two are able to stimulate their mind passively by listening to something interesting and educational, doing a fun activity like playing a game, or spending time connecting with family, thus filling your need for love and connection.

Unfortunately, many educational seminars are done entirely in Level Two. This is when all you need to do is show up for class, find a seat, and have the instructor speak *at* you instead of inviting you to actively participate. While you may glean some information from this style of teaching, if your mind remains in Level Two, and the instructor does nothing to raise your brain to a higher level, you will likely end up falling asleep. After all, Level Two is still a level of relaxation and recharging. (For tips on how to put on amazing, powerful, lucrative presentations, read my book *Being Boring Sucks, So Stop It!*)

Level Three Brain Activity: Rejuvenating Creation

This is what I call the first of the three *creation stages*. This is the level where your brain is able to create things that have to do with your hobbies, interests, and passions. For me, this is when I create dinner menus (I love to cook) or plan vacations and special occasions. I am not quite to the level where I can create life-changing products and services or brainstorm ways to improve my business, but I can still be creative in smaller ways. This helps fill the need for variety.

Level Four Brain Activity: Productive Creation

This is the level where I do business creation. I think of ways I can benefit the lives of others. I create new audio trainings, online programs, write new books, or fine-tune my outlines for upcoming classes. What you do in Level Four will help you progress in the various areas of your life, particularly financially, which fills the need for growth.

Level Five Brain Activity: Problem-Solving

You know when you are in Level Five because you feel like you can conquer the world. In Level Five, you are not only able to create but actually analyze and solve difficult problems. This is full-blast brain activity. I always make sure I am in Level Five when I am with my private mentoring clients because only in this level can I use my mind to help my students create plans of action for their business and life. I can accomplish anything that needs to get done. You will be the most productive in Level Five, which allows you to fulfill your needs for significance and contribution.

I recommend spending time in all five levels each day. Maybe while you are working, you are in Levels Four and Five. Perhaps when you come home to be with your family or friends, you then allow yourself some time in Levels Two and Three. You go to Level One as you unwind to go to sleep at night.

You may also find it beneficial to go straight to Level One after a prolonged period of time in Level Five. When I have a full day of seeing mentoring clients, I schedule time in between each appointment to spend in Level One so I can recharge my brain enough to get back to level Five when my next client arrives.

What does each level look like for you?

In your success journal, write down what each level of brain activity is like for you and make note of what honors you in each level. Balancing your time between each of the five levels will help you get *unstuck*.

Some personality types struggle to relax no matter how hard they try. Dr. Taylor Hartman created the Color Code Personality Test, which groups personalities into four major types, as follows:

Red

Red personalities are the power wielders of the world and are extremely task-oriented. They use logic, vision, and determination to quickly and effectively get things done. To a true red personality, task completion has little to do with emotion.

POSSIBLE STRENGTHS

Reds tend to be action-oriented, assertive, confident, decisive, determined, disciplined, independent, excellent leaders, highly logical in their thinking, productive, responsible, and proactive. Many company presidents and CEOs are red personalities because they know how to get things done.

POSSIBLE LIMITATIONS

Red personalities often have to be right. They can come across as harsh and critical, even when they don't mean to be. Reds can be cheap. They may make their work a higher priority than their personal relationships. They can be poor listeners and find it difficult to empathize. They can also exhibit controlling and domineering traits. True red personalities rarely take breaks because they are so driven, motivated, and task-oriented that they often believe relaxing is counterproductive.

Red personalities *especially* need to make blue screen time a priority, even if it is just a few minutes here and there. They often find that being outside in fresh air can be rejuvenating. Doing some of their work outside, such as working on their laptop at the park, can be the best of both worlds. They can be productive and get rejuvenated at the same time. It is especially important that they take time to eat and stay hydrated. They like to vacation at amusement parks because they can still be constantly moving. Going on as many rides as possible gives them a sense of accomplishment.

Blue

Life is a sequence of commitments for blue personalities. They are highly perfectionistic and can be distrusting and worry-prone. They are complex, highly logical, and often opinionated. Blue personalities tend to see life as a series of patterns. Thus, they are often extremely organized and excellent with numbers, data, and technology.

POSSIBLE STRENGTHS

Blues are steady, ordered, and enduring. Blues love with passion. They bring culture and dependency to society and home. They are highly committed and loyal. They are comfortable in creative environments. They strive to be the best they can be and are extremely organized.

POSSIBLE LIMITATIONS

Blues are often the most stubborn of the four personality types. They can be insecure and judgmental. Lacking trust, they find themselves resentful and unforgiving. They often fail to see the positive side of life. Wanting to be loved and accepted, they constantly seek understanding from others while refusing to understand and accept themselves. Because blues tend to be organizers, it often benefits them to do things someone organizes for them. Their form of blue screen time may include going to a restaurant so someone can organize, prepare, and clean up after their meal.

White

Motivated by peace and making sure everyone else is happy, white personalities will do anything to avoid confrontation. Their only demands from life are the things that make them and others feel comfortable. They are highly intuitive and empathetic. While they have a tendency to be shy and introverted, given the chance, white personalities often connect at a deeper level with people other than their own personality type.

POSSIBLE STRENGTHS

White personalities are kind, considerate, patient, accepting, and have very little ego. They are good at constructing thoughts that did not exist before just from careful listening and taking time to think things through. They are good at putting into words their feelings and the feelings of others.

POSSIBLE LIMITATIONS

White personalities don't commonly share what they are feeling, understanding or seeing. They won't express conflict. White personalities may be unwilling to set goals because they dislike working at someone else's pace. They can be somewhat self-deprecating. White personalities often recharge by being extremely still. They tend to enjoy taking warm baths during times when they won't be disturbed. They benefit from going to the spa, receiving massages, and spending time in nature. Often, when they go on vacation, they go somewhere remote where they can relax and do absolutely nothing.

Chapter 7: Blue Screen Time

Yellow

Yellow personalities are motivated by fun and excitement. They are here to have a great time. They are known for being spontaneous, optimistic, and love being the center of attention. Yellow personalities love to make friends and are often extremely extroverted.

POSSIBLE STRENGTHS

Yellow personalities are enthusiastic, persuasive, and tend to have a large network of friends and acquaintances. They are spontaneous in nature and always looking for something new to do. Yellows know how to liven up even the dullest moments, are fun to be around, and love to see the good in everything.

POSSIBLE LIMITATIONS

Yellow personalities develop friendships easily but can be self-centered, which prevents them from forming meaningful relationships. They often have a lot of friends but only on a superficial level. Yellows may have difficulty being productive. They often procrastinate and can be extremely flaky. They aren't the most reliable when it comes to keeping their commitments.

Yellow personality types recharge by doing fun things. It can be difficult for a yellow personality to go on vacation with a white personality because the white personality will usually want to just sit, relax, and read a book, while the yellow personality will want to explore and do fun activities. Yellows want to have as many new and fun experiences as possible. Much like red personalities, yellow personalities often choose amusement parks as great places to recharge and unwind. The parks are lots of fun and keep the yellow types constantly moving and interacting with other people.

"But, Eric, what do I do if I'm married to a completely different personality type? What if we want to go on vacation and meet all our needs?"

My wife and I are polar opposites when it comes to personality types. I am mostly red/yellow, and she is mostly white/blue. We've found that cruises and all-inclusive resorts tend to work best for us because we get to do a fun, exciting, and engaging activity or excursion in the morning (which appeases my red and yellow personalities), have some relaxing down time in the afternoon (which appeases my wife's white personality), then enjoy an amazing dinner and watch a great show (which, of course, are all organized and produced by the cruise line or resort, which appeases her blue personality).

"But, Eric, what do I do if I'm *mentally stuck,* if I just can't seem to get my brain to work?"

This can happen if a project you are working on requires more mental work than physical work. Writers often experience this in the form of writer's block. If you feel *mentally stuck*, tap into intuition and ask, "Intuition, am I experiencing a *timing issue*?"

Timing issues occur when we arrive at a place in our project we are not yet ready to complete. I experienced this several times while writing this book. I realized I had not yet had the experiences necessary to learn the lessons I had to include.

If intuition suggests you are experiencing a timing issue, set the project aside and allow the ideas to come when the time is right. Some lessons cannot be forced.

If intuition suggests you are *not* experiencing a timing issue, it may be necessary to grit your teeth and *burn your britches.*

CHAPTER 8
BURN YOUR BRITCHES

What does the term "whatever it takes" mean to you? What does being a "whatever it takes person" mean to you?

Have you ever heard the phrase "burn your bridges behind you"? This phrase is common within the personal development industry, but what does it mean?

Imagine you are trying to get to a magical watering hole, which we'll call "The Fountain of Youth." If you drink of its waters, all your greatest desires become reality. In order to get to it, you must cross a number of challenging obstacles, including a rickety old bridge to the other side of the mountain, where The Fountain of Youth is located. On the other side of the bridge, you must still overcome a number of obstacles. That means you have to stretch yourself outside your comfort zone to reach the fountain of your dreams.

After crossing to the other side, you decide to destroy the bridge so there is no way you can turn back before reaching The Fountain of Youth. You pull out your lighter, set the bridge on fire, and watch it burn. You've literally burned your bridge behind you, making it impossible for you to take a "chicken exit" by turning back before you reach your destination.

Throughout your journey to achieve your goals, you may have done several things that could qualify as "burning your bridges behind you." Perhaps you invested in training seminars. Maybe you quit a full-time job to start a business. You may have hired a high-end mentor for a large sum of money to help lead you to success. Unfortunately, there is still a major problem. Even though you eliminated your chicken exits and made it so you can no longer go backward, nothing is preventing you from sitting down right where you are, crossing your arms and legs and saying, "I'm not going any farther! I'm staying right here! I am done!"

The sad truth is that many people do this, even after investing in training seminars, quitting their full-time jobs to start a business, and hiring high-end mentors for large sums of money. A lot of people think that, by attending one seminar or hiring one mentor, everything in their life will magically change. Then they make excuses to reject other opportunities to further grow themselves.

"I've already invested all I possibly could into this one mentoring program, so I don't have the money to do any more."

"I'm already spending a lot of time with this mentor, so any time other opportunities present themselves, I'm just going to say I don't have time."

Their results don't change much because, as we discussed in Chapter 2, they aren't willing to jump in with both feet. Thus they stay *stuck*.

What if, instead of burning your bridges, you decided to burn your *britches*?

Let's say you've crossed the bridge and are now on the side of the mountain where The Fountain of Youth is located. Let's say you have a magical lighter whose fire can only be put out by water from The Fountain of Youth. What would happen if you used it to light your britches on fire? You would run as fast as you could to The Fountain of Youth because you wouldn't want to burn your bum off! You wouldn't care how many obstacles you encountered or challenges you needed to overcome along the way. You would do *what-*

Chapter 8: Burn Your Britches

ever it took to reach The Fountain of Youth as quickly as humanly possible because you don't want to lose your bum, which is what would happen if you *didn't* reach The Fountain of Youth.

The biggest difference between the successful and the mediocre is that the successful are willing (figuratively) to *burn their britches*.

For clarification, this is only an analogy. I am *not* telling you to literally light your pants on fire. (Isn't it ridiculous that I have to clarify this?)

"Burning your britches" is a term we use in my company, which simply means do whatever it takes to (figuratively) light a fire under yourself and get going as quickly as possible.

In Chapter 5, I shared my experience of borrowing nearly $5,000 for a mentoring program while I was still on welfare and $25,000 to work with a mentor one-on-one. Fast forward two more years, and things were going quite well. My wife and I were living in a million-dollar home, I bought my wife two of her dream cars, our company was growing and expanding, but I felt in my heart I was capable of more. As good as things were, I still wasn't getting the results I desired, which meant I wasn't able to reach as many lives as I needed to reach. I was *stuck*.

I was invited to attend a live event hosted by a millionaire mentor about an hour away from my house. I was impressed by what I saw, heard, and felt, so I arranged to meet with this mentor inside his home. After getting to know him and sharing with him the challenges I was facing in my business, I asked what it would take for him to mentor me one-on-one over the next year.

The number he wrote was far beyond anything I expected.

He told me it would cost $100,000 for him to mentor me for a year, and my jaw dropped.

"Are you in?" he asked.

"Let me check," I responded. I checked in with my intuition, asking, "Is it right for me to move forward with this mentor?"

I received an immediate "Yes!"

"I am in," I told him, trepidatiously.

"Awesome," he replied. "How soon can you come up with the funds?"

"Let me check," I said again.

"Intuition," I thought. "How soon can we come up with the funds to work with this mentor?"

"Within a week," was the answer.

"One week?" I almost burst out laughing. I had never earned $100,000 in a single week at that point.

Cautiously, I responded, "Give me a week."

"Fantastic," the mentor congratulated me with a high five. "I know you can do it!"

I was terrified. I am a man of my word, and I had just given my word to generate $100,000 in seven days for this gentleman I felt could help me become a millionaire. How was I supposed to accomplish the seemingly impossible?

I racked my mind for answers, utilizing the tools you learned in Chapter 4. How could I generate $100,000 in seven days?

I ended up doing something I do not recommend. I took out several business capital loans. Business capital loans are different from traditional loans, which allow you to make monthly payments for a number of years until the loan is paid in full. Business capital loans typically begin at forty percent interest with a six-month payback term instead of several years. Rather than a monthly payment, payments were automatically deducted from my bank account every business day, meaning, with the exception of weekends, approximately $650 was yanked from my bank account each day, which totaled more than $14,000 per month. If, at any time, my bank account went negative, I would owe an additional $5,000.

While these figures may seem devastating to some, I realized I had two choices: Watching my bank account get smaller each day could cripple me, or it could light a fire under me, get me moving, and create a return on my investment.

Thankfully, I chose the latter.

I showed up early to every appointment with this mentor, and, like a sponge, I soaked up all the knowledge I could from him.

A few months later, I was planning my first, three-day transformational seminar. Up to that point, my company had only hosted single-day events. Because we had grown and expanded so much, we needed the extra two days to impart everything we wanted our audience to know.

We titled the class *Master Creator*.

I wanted this event to be a hit, so I invested all I had into making it successful. I was putting it all on the line. If the event was a success, it would put our company on the map. If not, we would likely have to shut our doors.

Two weeks before the event, my mentor asked me to show him my business model of everything I planned to do at Master Creator. I went through my outline of topics, the offers I would make, the price point of each of my offers —and I cringed when I saw his look of disapproval.

"Eric," he started, "You can do things like this, but you won't have nearly as big of an impact unless you do it like *this*." He crossed out my business model and wrote a completely different one.

"Are you kidding me?" I thought. "You're telling me all this *now*? Just *two weeks* before the event?"

I was tempted to ignore the counsel my mentor gave me that day. It would have been much easier to continue to do things as I had always done them. This new business model would stretch me far outside my comfort zone, especially in the remaining two weeks before the event. But I had burned my britches by investing so much into this mentorship, so I decided to implement everything he suggested.

I realized after the event that, had we kept to our original plan, we would have lost everything.

Because I implemented the new business model, we generated more than $115,000 from the event.

I'll never forget the feeling that came over me as I looked at the numbers and realized all the lives we had forever transformed because we were willing to burn our britches. We lit a fire under ourselves, implemented what our mentors taught us to do, and turned an investment of $100,000 into millions over the next couple of years.

If you feel *stuck,* there's a good chance you haven't completely burned your britches.

"But Eric, I've invested tens of thousands of dollars into a mentoring program. What do you mean I haven't burned my britches?"

You may have invested a lot of time and money, but ask yourself if doing so was truly enough to actually light a fire under you and cause you to become a "whatever it takes" person.

(Side note: when I mention being a "whatever it takes" person, that is inherently followed by "as long as it is legal, moral, and ethical.")

The act of hiring mentors will not change your life. Mentors can't force you to be successful. Mentors can lead you to The Fountain of Youth, but they cannot force you to drink from it. That part is up to you.

What does it mean to you to burn your britches? In what ways have you been unwilling to do so?

Answer the following in your success journal:

I have been unwilling to…

My unwillingness to do what I just wrote down is costing me…

I must burn my britches by… .

The rewards that will come to me as a result of doing so include…

I now 100 percent commit to doing this by (write a date)…

As you answer these questions, you may think of all the ways burning your britches will be uncomfortable or painful. The subconscious mind is designed to keep you alive; thus it does everything it can to avoid potentially painful situations.

Consider that for a moment.

How many people do you know who are overweight and would love to slim down and get fit? They don't like how they look or feel, and they know they would look and feel considerably better if they transformed their body. Unfortunately, if they believe the process of transformation will be more painful than the pain of being overweight, they will never begin the process.

If you desire to become a millionaire, and understand that one of the fastest ways of doing so is to start a business, but you subconsciously believe the process of getting started and running a business will be too much hassle, you will never do it. You will remain *stuck*.

Thankfully, change is usually less painful than we believe it will be.

I remained *stuck* at my heaviest weight for several years because I believed I would need to deprive myself, do endless hours of exercise, and torture myself to achieve a new body. It wasn't until I finally realized the process of change could actually be even more enjoyable than the process of staying where I was that I finally transformed my body.

Keep in mind that things are only uncomfortable until they are *not*.

Have you ever started a new exercise program? After the first day or two, you likely experienced a period of soreness. You may have asked yourself why you began the routine in the first place. But after a few days, the soreness subsided, and you were able to proceed with the exercise. The same principle applies to business, new relationships, or any other process that causes growth. Things will only be uncomfortable until they are *not*.

"But, Eric, what if I burn my britches and put everything on the line, and everything blows up in my face? What then?"

It might.

You might do everything right, and things still don't turn out the way you hoped. As difficult as this might be, you may be on the verge of experiencing your ultimate test.

Being Stuck Sucks, So Stop It!

CHAPTER 9
OVERCOMING OPPOSITION

The following text is taken from a recording I did on my phone while in the middle of my ultimate test. It is written as it was spoken, word for word, without edits, except to clarify the intention of what I was saying. This is extremely personal; it is me at my most vulnerable. I share some of the trials I was going through and the lessons I learned along the way. I have included it in this book so that, when you go through your own ultimate test, you will have something to relate to.

I also discuss deep, spiritual insight I received according to my personal beliefs, so please do not read this section if you are someone who would take offense at that. Please only read this section from a place of unconditional love.

The next several pages will be from the recording.

Hello, my friend. This is Eric Bailey. I am not in the recording studio. I am sitting here in my bed. It's after one o'clock in the morning, and I just felt impressed to make this recording. I've spent a lot of time over the past few weeks, probably more time than I would care to admit, just lying here in bed, sometimes with the covers over my head, because I've given in to a lot of fear over the past couple of months. I have faced some of the absolute fiercest,

fiercest opposition. And it's really... it's really been an interesting past couple of months.

What's been going on is, there is a group of individuals who, for whatever reason, has taken it upon themselves to try to tear me down. To try to tarnish whatever reputation I may have had. To try to destroy my business. And basically, what they have been doing is they've started a social media group, and they've invited a lot of people to join with them. And in this group, they tear down my name. They say that I'm this horrible person, that I'm a fraud, that I'm a liar, that I'm a manipulator, that I said all of these horrible things—which I never said—and did all these terrible things—which I never did. And it's been a really interesting journey over the past couple of months.

And again, I'm not quite sure why I'm making this recording. Hopefully, maybe one day, well, I'll end up releasing this. I don't have a script. I don't have an outline or anything. This is just me talking. But I've learned so many interesting things over the past couple of months—through all the opposition, through all the fear, through all the doubts, through these moments of absolute chaos and heartbreak.

As I've come to find that people that I deemed very close friends, that I loved, that... that were students of mine... now tearing my name apart and saying that... fabricating so many stories about me. I honestly—I have no idea why they would do such things, but I've come to learn that, through all of our trials come amazing lessons, and so with your permission, I want to just share some of the things that I've been learning over the past couple of months as I've gone through this fierce opposition. I want to warn you that I will probably be going into some very personal, as well as some possibly very spiritual, topics, and so if you're the type of person that gets offended at spiritual topics or will get offended by me sharing some

Chapter 9: Overcoming Opposition

really personal things with you, then I recommend not continuing to listen to this recording. But one of the things that I've learned is that our trials are only there to make us stronger. And I know that sounds really cliché. I mean, we hear that all the time. We hear that our trials are just there to help us build character and just there to help us build faith, but it's really fascinating how this works. You probably know how when we exercise, when we use our muscles—for example, when a person goes to the gym and lifts weights, what's happening is that resistance is actually tearing that muscle apart, tearing the very fiber of the muscle basically to shreds. And what then happens is the body will then rebuild that muscle just slightly bigger and slightly stronger. Over the past couple of months—I'll be honest: I felt absolutely torn to shreds.

Something about me is that my love language is words of affirmation. And if you're familiar with the love languages—whatever a person's love language is—the opposite of their love language tends to be what hurts the most. For example, those whose love language is loving touch: if they were to receive a hurtful touch—if someone were to physically abuse them, for example—that would be, I mean, more than physically devastating. That would be emotionally and mentally devastating for them as well.

For me, with my love language being words of affirmation, words of criticism and just negative feedback are extremely hurtful to me, especially as I really do my best to serve people with all my heart. People who come to me for B.E.S.T. treatments, or come to my classes, or hire me as a mentor... I really, really care about them, and I really want them to succeed. And I really want to do as good of a job as I possibly can.

And part of the reason that I want to see them succeed is because of my ego. It's because there's a big part of me that wants to receive those glowing testimonials and to see just how far they've come (in) the time that they have been working with me. And, you know, I've received countless testimonials. Dozens and dozens of testimonials of students of mine, people that have come to my seminars or that I've mentored, or have received B.E.S.T. treatments from me, saying these amazing results that they've had. And one of my weaknesses, like I said, is having that ego and allowing myself to kind of have my ego stroked when I receive those testimonials, those positive reviews. And it allows me to think, "Wow, look; look how great I am. Look how amazing of a mentor, or B.E.S.T. practitioner, or trainer I am if I can cause such powerful transformations in people. And so, when people who at one time were giving me these glowing testimonials then turn around and just say these horrible, horrible things about me, it really hurts.

And one of the things that I wish I could say isn't true but it is... I allow it to get to me way too much. I take things like that way too personally. And something that I found, that I've had to come to terms with, is that whenever a person speaks negatively about another person—whenever someone judges another person or whenever we see something that we don't like in someone else—it's really just a reflection of what we don't like in ourselves.

And having said that, I don't want you to listen to this recording and think that I'm just shirking responsibility, because I'm not. I've... I've made countless mistakes, some that I... that I'm still paying the price for. Things that I... that I still regret. Personal mistakes, business mistakes, marriage mistakes, mistakes with my children. And so, please don't think that I'm just saying, "Oh, you know, it's all on them," because, no, I've made a lot of mistakes, and I have hurt a lot of people. Not trying to hurt them, but because of my ignorance and because of just dumb things that I've done, I have. I've hurt a lot of people. But again, people come back and say things that, you know, say that I've said things, I've done things that I didn't say. It's

Chapter 9: Overcoming Opposition

been like… they've said really hurtful things to me. But, again, I take solace in knowing that a lot of it isn't about me. A lot of it is simply them working through the very trials that are eating at them.

Something that I've come to learn is that a judgment against someone is nothing more than a deflection of an open soul wound. And what that means is all of us have emotional wounds. A lot of us have emotional wounds stemming from way back into the early days of our childhood. And what tends to happen is the soul wounds will kind of scab over. And so, they will partially heal, to the point where we don't feel them all the time, but something will happen that will remind us of the pain of one of those soul wounds. And when that happens, our natural tendency is to try to deflect attention away from that pain. And we do that by forming a judgment against someone else.

And it's fascinating. One of the things that I've seen as I've been on this journey of becoming a mentor, of starting my own company, of working with people on a very personal, very powerful, one-on-one basis is that, the more good that a person sets out to do in this world, the fiercer the opposition tends to be.

It still amazes me that the man that I worship as my Savior is also the most cursed name ever in existence. People take this person's name in vain more so than they curse any other name. And it just boggles my mind. I mean, here's this perfect man. This man that walked the earth, whose sole intention was to love other people and to serve other people, and who actually died for us so that we could one day become more like Him, and that we could be forgiven of our… of our sins and our imperfections. And yet, this very man, ironically and technically, is a convicted felon and was given the death penalty. I mean, have you ever thought about that? I mean, obviously He did nothing wrong. He was totally innocent. But technically, He was convicted of blasphemy or whatever else they decided they wanted to accuse Him of, and He was given the death penalty, which at that time was crucifixion.

And a person who is a total nonbeliever may look at that, and he may scratch his head, and he might say, "So, wait a second, you're telling me that you look up to and you actually worship a man who is a convicted felon and was given the death penalty?" And the answer is, "Yep, I sure do! I worship Him as my Lord and my Savior, and I view Him as the very Son of God." And He's a man that I am continuously striving to become more like, and striving to emulate.

Now, obviously, I could never, ever even come close. I couldn't even think of comparing myself to Him, so please don't think that's what I'm trying to do here. But with all of this opposition, with everything that's been going on, as difficult as it's been, I just keep picturing Him in my mind. And I just keep imagining Him saying those words, "Father, forgive them, for they know not what they do."

I had a friend send me a message today, just earlier today. And she said something that really made me think of this. She basically said, "Eric, it's time for you to stop putting so much energy into this opposition that you've been facing. It's time for you to stop sending that energy." Which, of course, she reminded me of the principle that whatever we focus on expands. And she said, "It's time to start letting go of the hurt you have been holding onto."

It's time to start forgiving all those people who have been hurting me and to start loving them and empathizing with them in all the trials that they're going through, because, obviously, they are experiencing some major pain I probably couldn't even fathom—that I probably couldn't even understand. And obviously, all these judgments that are coming against me and my company and—and it isn't just me, they're attacking a lot of, several different, mentors. They seem to be attacking mentors in general. And so, it isn't just me that they are attacking.

Chapter 9: Overcoming Opposition

But I mean the fact that anyone would purposely set out to attack any one person or any group of people, to me, again tells me that they are probably going through some really difficult times. Maybe they're going through some financial difficulties. Maybe they're struggling in their marriage. Maybe, I don't know—maybe something happened, and they're just going through some depression and so they're coping with it. And the only way that they know...

Now, does that make it any easier for me? Maybe not; but maybe it does. And, again, does it have to be easier for me? No, because this isn't about me, and that's one of the biggest things that I'm learning right now. I'm learning to overcome my massive, massive ego that wants to make everything about me.

My wife is one the most amazing mentors I've ever, ever known, and she's so, so talented, and she's so gifted. And I'm so thankful for everything that she does to help me when I go through moments of opposition because she's so blunt, and she's so loving, and she basically, finally, not too long ago, just looked me in the eyes and said, "Eric, when are you going to stop giving yourself so much credit and stop thinking that this is all about you? This isn't about you, Eric! This is about them dealing with whatever it is that they're dealing with!"

And I was reminded of a quote of something that I had said in another one of my CDs, which is that the brightest lights offend the most cockroaches. Now think about that for a moment. Have you ever—maybe you were visiting another country or maybe just some really dirty apartment or something—have you ever been in a dark room and then turned on a light and seen cockroaches scatter? It's really, really gross, so I hope you don't live in an area where you have cockroaches. But for the first year and a half of my marriage, my wife and I actually lived in a certain city in Utah where there were cockroaches. And we kept our apartment clean, and we didn't live in the slums or anything like that. But because cockroaches were, you know, really common in that area, occasionally we would turn on the lights in the middle of the night going to use the bathroom, and there would be some cockroaches that would scurry because they liked the darkness. They didn't want the light. The light offended them... .

It's fascinating to see just how many of the greatest men and women who have ever walked the earth were also some of the most judged and criticized and hated people to ever walk the earth. We recently—just yesterday—celebrated Martin Luther King Jr. Day, and Martin Luther King Jr., of course, was an amazing civil rights activist. And he helped to secure equal rights for African-Americans, and he did just unbelievably amazing things in our country. And yet he was... he was killed. He was murdered. He was hated because of the great work that he was doing, because of all of the feathers that he ruffled.

Again, I think of Jesus, the greatest man who ever walked this earth whose name is taken in vain so often. I think of so many other people that really stood up for what they believed in. And because they did so, it ruffled so many feathers. And people decided that they wanted to take it upon themselves to try to stop them, to try to shut them down.

If you are going through anything even remotely similar to this—it could be that you are wanting to start a business and yet you fear judgment from your parents or from a spouse or from coworkers or from neighbors or friends; whatever it is that might be going on in your life—my friend, please, please, please know that you're not alone. Please know that your opposition is only a temporary thing. It may seem like it's going to last a lifetime. It may seem like this is how it's going to be forever and that there's no way to overcome it, but please know that the

Chapter 9: Overcoming Opposition

opposition that you've been experiencing is really, really, truly just for your good.

And, again, I know that's much easier to say than it is to actually believe or experience. And to be honest, with everything that I've been going through, I have to keep reminding myself of this principle over and over and over again just to get myself through everything that I've been experiencing. But, again, that old cliché still holds true that opposition truly does make us stronger. And it's always right before the greatest rewards come our way that the opposition tends to be the strongest.

Another thing that I have struggled with in all of this is I'm extremely guilty of basing my personal value—my self-worth—on my outside results. Something that I've been very proud of is, I was able to become successful with my business pretty quickly. In my very first full calendar year of owning my own business, I made a six-figure income. And it's only continued to increase every single year. I mean, we've broken records so many times in our company, and then it's grown so quickly, and I've been guilty a lot of times of hiding behind some of the financial success that I've had. Even when, deep down, I was really hurting because of the failures that I had.

Something that I still struggle with is my weight. My ideal weight is 160 pounds, and I got up to 246 just over a year ago. And I hired a world-class personal trainer, and he helped me to release several pounds. But then, because of a lot of stress that I went through, I gained a lot of it back. And my weight has just kept yo-yoing back and forth, and I'd lose some weight, and then I gained it back. And I lose the weight again and gain it back. And I've been so frustrated with myself because of these so-called failures that I've based my self-worth off of my failures rather than my successes.

And there have been many times when I've based my self-worth off of the amount of money I've had in the bank. Meaning if I had just recently made some sort of huge investment and the numbers in the bank were low, that would cause my self-worth to get quite low. If I just made a whole bunch of sales and I had a lot of money in the bank, then my self-worth would go up.

And it's frustrating because I teach this. I teach people that results and money and success and happiness follow personal value, not the other way around. And something that I've been working to achieve is being enough, regardless of my outside results, regardless of my outside circumstances. Meaning, whether everyone in the world hates me and says that I'm a fraud or a manipulator or whatever, or everyone in the entire world loves me and looks up to me and wants to learn from me, I'm striving to be enough on the inside, regardless of the size of my house, regardless of the size of my bank account, regardless of how many people attend my classes, regardless of anything on the outside. I'm striving to be enough on the inside, and that's my invitation to you as well. Is it easier said than done? Yeah, but I know who I am.

About a year and a half ago, I had a very, very powerful personal experience; a personal revelation, if you will, given to me in which I was told the type of life that I'm supposed to live. I was told the type of financial success that I'm supposed to achieve, the church responsibilities that I'm supposed to have, the physique that I'm supposed to achieve, the family life that I'm supposed to create, the faith that I'm supposed to have… and it scared the crap out of me because it's like—wait! I'm supposed to achieve all of *that*? How? I'm one person! The most important thing is that I keep moving forward and that I pick myself back up every time I stumble and I fall. And I don't know about you, but I stumble and I fall an awful lot.

And it seems like every time I take two steps forward, I take a step back, and then two steps forward and one step back. And then maybe a couple more steps back, and then maybe a couple of

Chapter 9: Overcoming Opposition

steps forward, and then a few steps back again. And I keep falling and stumbling and running into roadblock after roadblock after roadblock.

And thankfully, I once heard that the biggest difference between successful people and unsuccessful people isn't that successful people don't have hardships. It isn't that successful people don't have challenges or trials. It's that successful people simply get themselves back up, pick themselves back up every single time that they fall. They don't allow themselves to accept defeat when they fail.

Failure doesn't mean defeat. Failure simply means that you have a chance to learn. You have a chance to grow. And you have an opportunity to overcome a trial and become stronger.

So, my friend, my challenge for you (and, of course, my challenge for me as well) is to continue to be enough on the inside so that, regardless of what's happening on the outside, you can still keep moving forward and you can still have that confidence and that self-love, which will help you to overcome literally any fear.

Love and fear are polar opposites. They cannot coexist. And so, if you allow yourself to be filled with love, fear cannot exist in your mind. It simply can't. Love chases fear away. And love for yourself is going to be what helps you to get through those trials. And so, what I'm going to start doing is telling myself that I love myself. I love me. I love myself, and I like myself. I like myself. I love myself. I like myself, and I love myself. Even when I look in the mirror and my body isn't quite what I want it to be, I can still like myself, and I can still love myself. And I can know exactly who I truly am. And if that's who I truly am, then what does it matter what other people think of me or what other people say about me? And if I can simply view all of my trials as opportunities for growth, then how much easier will it be to get through those trials?

If I can see everyone that seems to oppose me as the Savior in disguise, then how much easier will it be for me to love that person, to love those people who are opposing me? If I can choose to see everything that they do—every "negative" thing that they say about me or do to try to destroy or shut my company down—as acts of love in disguise, and I take responsibility for how I show up, I could choose to be better.

I could choose to continue to let my ego dictate my actions and continue to wallow in self-pity when those moments come. Or, when I get a negative review about me or about my company, I could choose to, again, see each and every one of those people as the Savior in disguise. As someone who absolutely has my best interest at heart and is helping me to overcome my biggest fear, which is that of not being good enough and the fear of failure.

So my invitation to you, my friend, is to do the same; to see those who oppose you as the Savior in disguise. To see all of your trials as opportunities for growth. To use your agency to choose love, to choose happiness, to choose joy—and choose into those things which bring those feelings.

My friend, you are not alone. Please know how much you are loved. Even though it may seem like the entire world is against you at times, please know that I'm rooting for you. I want you to succeed, and I know you can!

***

As difficult as it is to experience an ultimate test, it may be the best thing that ever happens to you. Your ultimate test may be the refiner's fire you need to stop being *stuck* and become the person you are here to become.

Chapter 9: Overcoming Opposition

"But, Eric, my ultimate test is worse than I ever feared it would be. What if I just don't feel like 'looking on the bright side' or 'trying to learn a lesson?'"

When you feel this way, it is very possible you could be experiencing one of the six stages of *depression*.

Every day, millions of people around the world experience major bouts of depression. In my healthcare practice, people often come to me because they feel sluggish, constantly tired, and have lost their motivation. When I ask them about depression, they seem surprised.

"I'm a go-getter," they respond. "I help people overcome challenges in their own lives. How could I possibly have depression?"

Because depression can rear its ugly head in many different ways, those experiencing it often do so without realizing it. The information in this section is designed to help you identify and recognize the six stages of depression so that, accompanied by competent medical and psychological help, you can better survive and overcome the symptoms if you ever experience them in your own life.

Each stage of depression comes with its own unique set of challenges and action steps. The action steps utilized by an individual in one stage of depression will usually be inappropriate for someone in another stage.

The first stage is the deepest stage of depression. All motivation is lost. For a person in Stage One, survival is the only thing on their mind. In extreme cases, they may experience suicidal thoughts because they feel hopeless. Because of this, there is no desire to do anything that would bring any amount of happiness or overcome the depression. It doesn't help when others say things like, "Just snap out of it." Telling a person in Stage One to "just snap out of it" can cause them to sink deeper into depression because, in addition to being depressed, they now feel shame for feeling the way they feel.

The action step during this stage is *honoring and validating your feelings*. There is no need to feel guilty or shameful for being depressed. This is where a lot of mentors and coaches get stuck because, after all, people hire us to help them overcome their challenges, so it can seem scary and downright depressing when we have our own challenges. We feel like we have no right to help others through their problems when we don't have everything figured out for ourselves.

If you find yourself in Stage One, honor and validate your feelings by planting both feet firmly on the ground, shoulder width apart, and shouting, "I feel depressed, and it sucks!"

Give yourself permission to feel the way you do. You may find the cloud of depression begin to dissipate once you acknowledge its existence.

If you understand the concept of *chakras*, note that a person in Stage One usually has a blocked root chakra. Planting the feet and validating the feelings of depression help unblock this chakra, which is associated with your sense of safety and security.

The second stage is where you "want to want" to feel better. Does that make sense? You aren't ready for actively *trying* to feel better, but you do wish you could feel better as long as you can do something *passive*.

If you find yourself in Stage Two, watch a funny video or listen to uplifting music (both are passive activities) to at least get your head above water and start smiling.

A person in Stage Two usually has a blocked sacral chakra, and doing something passive will help them feel nurtured, thus unblocking this chakra.

The third stage is when you *want* to feel better; you are tired of feeling depressed and are ready for a change. Because it may be difficult to find something in the present to be happy about at this stage, choose something in the future to look forward to—it could be a vacation, a special occasion, or something you can create. Doing so can spark a wave of creativity to help pull you out of Stage Three.

A person in Stage Three usually has blocked solar plexus and heart chakras. The action steps described in this section help unblock these chakras.

The fourth stage is when a person is ready to reach out for help and begin to feel better. It is critical that you do not try to overcome Stage Four on your own. Reach out to loved ones who can help boost your spirits, and also seek professional help. Use intuition to seek the help that would be right for you, be it with medical professionals, psychiatric professionals, B.E.S.T. practitioners, mentors, timeline breakthrough practitioners, hypnotherapists, or whatever is appropriate for your individual circumstances. You must use your *voice* to ask for help and explain what is going on in your life. Doing so will help unblock the throat chakra, the center of communication, typically blocked in Stage Four.

If you or someone you know needs additional resources, send an email to ClientServices@FeelWellLiveWell.com and let our team know that you or a loved one is suffering from depression and would like additional help. We can put you in touch with licensed professionals to assist you, usually at no charge.

The fifth stage takes place after getting outside help. This is when you *get moving*. Physical activity, especially in fresh air, invigorates the mind and releases endorphins in the body. Find an exercise program that works for you, even if it's simply going for a five-minute walk in nature. Exercise and time spent in nature help open the third eye chakra, the center of intuition, typically blocked in Stage Five.

The sixth stage is when you are finally ready to *look for lessons* to learn from the events that triggered the depression. As you know, every experience in our lives is designed to teach us certain lessons. Pain without learning equals *suffering*, but pain *with* learning leads to *breakthrough*.

If you find yourself in Stage Six, ask yourself what positive lessons you can learn and retain from the experiences you have gone through. Write these lessons down and allow yourself to feel gratitude for the experiences you have had. Depression can be dispelled with pure gratitude.

The crown chakra—the connection to our spirituality—is the typical block in Stage Six. To unblock it, feel and experience sincere gratitude in life.

It is also important in any stage to shift your *physical state*.

What does a depressed person's body language look like? To demonstrate this concept, right now shift your body to look like it would if you were experiencing extreme depression. When this happens, the shoulders, arms, and head hang low, and everything seems to droop. Again, put your body into this state right now. Notice how you feel when you spend thirty seconds or more with your body in this state.

Now shift your body to look like it would if you had just achieved the biggest goal on your dream board. If you can't think of one off the top of your head, imagine that a fortune 500 company saw something you posted on your social media page and loved it so much they want to pay you $10 million right now for the use of your "inspirational quote." How different would your body language be?

When you feel excited and confident, you stand up tall, your shoulders go back, your chest pumps, and you hold your head high. Again, put your body into this state right now and keep it like this for thirty seconds or more while imagining you just achieved the biggest goal on your dream board. Notice how much different you feel in this state versus when you exhibited depressed body language.

The moment you notice any stage of depression, change the state of your body.

Write the following in your success journal:

"I easily recognize the six stages of depression and immediately take appropriate action. I immediately change the state of my body and act according to the stage I am in."

Now place your hand over your heart and declare, "I am amazing!"

Stages one through three of depression take place below heart level. Stages four through six take place above heart level. If you feel yourself going into a lower stage of depression, the following heart meditation script may be useful. I suggest you make a recording of yourself reading it out loud. When you feel yourself going below heart level, go somewhere where you can be totally alone and undisturbed (i.e., your bedroom), get into a comfortable position, and listen to the heart meditation. Because you will hear your own voice without your lips moving, your subconscious mind will automatically accept it as your "inner voice."

Heart Meditation

Take a deep breath in and exhale through your mouth. And as you do, focus your breathing on your heart. Breathe deeply into your heart. Close your eyes, and focus all of your attention on your heart. Go now and allow yourself to be one with your heart. And as you allow yourself to breathe deeply into your heart and be one with your heart, feel the strength, power, and beauty of your being.

Allow yourself to feel the beating of your heart and allow yourself to feel gratitude that your heart is beating. That you are alive. Consider that for a moment. You are alive; you have a body—you have a brilliant body that moves and functions and sees and hears and tastes and smells and connects. This body was given to you as a gift from your Maker.

And now, as you continue your heart-focused breathing, remember a moment in your life during which you were totally and completely grateful. Perhaps this was a moment you are proud of. Perhaps this was a moment that you met someone or connected with someone. Breathe into your heart while focusing on your heart and allow yourself to feel that wonderful, powerful moment, that magical moment. Feel how sacred that moment was and is. And allow yourself to feel total gratitude for that moment. What a gift that moment was! And go to that moment now.

Step fully into that moment and be present in it. See what you saw, hear what you heard, feel what you felt in that moment. Allow yourself to smile and be fully present. Notice your breathing. How do you breathe when you are in total and complete gratitude? Celebration is the highest form of gratitude, so allow yourself to internally celebrate this moment and all the other moments like this one.

Fill yourself up with this feeling of gratitude and celebration. Then press gently on your heart to anchor this feeling in. Lock in this feeling of gratitude and celebration so that, from this moment forward, all you need to do is gently press on your heart to instantly and automatically feel gratitude and celebration.

Now think of a second moment in your life you can truly celebrate. A moment that allows you to feel totally and completely grateful. And fully step into that moment. See what you saw, hear what you heard, and feel what you felt when you were in that moment. Notice your breathing as you continue to breathe deeply into your heart, feeling total gratitude and celebration. Breathe that feeling in deeply through your heart, and press gently on your heart to anchor that feeling in. That beautiful feeling of gratitude and celebration from that special, magical moment. Fill yourself with that sacred feeling.

Continue breathing deeply into your heart and think of a third moment in your life during which you felt completely grateful and thankful. Think of the beauty of that moment and all that moment has done for your life. And go now to that moment and feel what you felt in that moment, see what you saw, and hear what you heard.

Allow yourself to be filled with gratitude and celebration. Feel the love in your heart as you continue breathing deeply into your heart. Become totally and completely present in that moment, allowing that feeling to spread throughout your entire body. Gently press your heart to anchor in that gratitude and celebration so that, from this moment forward, any time you press your heart, you are filled with that incredible feeling of gratitude and celebration.

Continuing in this state—stay out of your head and stay in your heart—continue to breathe deeply into your heart, feeling grateful. Consider the incomplete equation in your life, the unfinished business that has showed up in your life multiple times. And in this beautiful state of gratitude, ask yourself what you need to focus on to complete the equation and solve the issue. Stay in your heart, and simply allow ideas to flow through you. Your heart knows the answer. Your heart knows all the answers.

Ask yourself, "What do I need to focus on, remember, or do to resolve this once and for all in my life?" Allow the answer to come to you. Breathe the answer in and allow yourself to feel completely grateful for that answer.

Celebrate having received this answer in your mind. Now speak these words: "I am confident! I've got this!" And keeping this state of gratitude, celebration, and confidence, open your eyes, write the answer down, and go make it happen.

As you stay in your heart, you will be more aligned with your purpose. The more aligned you become with your purpose, the more aligned you will be with *the three pillars of growth*.

Being Stuck Sucks, So Stop It!

CHAPTER 10
THREE PILLARS OF GROWTH

Not long ago I had the privilege of taking my wife to San Francisco for a vacation. If you've ever been to San Francisco, you know that one of the most popular tourist destinations is the Golden Gate Bridge. We visited it our first morning in the city. As we took pictures and spent several minutes admiring the incredible structure, I noticed it was held in place by three main pillars: one on each end of the bridge and one in the middle. These three pillars have held this enormous bridge in place in all types of weather for more than eight decades since construction, all while over 10 million people every year cross it on foot, on their bikes, or in cars and buses.

Just as this world-famous bridge has three pillars that hold it in place, we have three pillars in our lives that comprise our main areas of personal growth: the body, the mind, and the soul.

Most people make the mistake of focusing on only one pillar at a time. For example, those who want to reduce their weight usually adopt some form of diet and exercise plan, focusing only on the *body pillar*. As important as diet and exercise are, alone, they often fail to produce lasting results—as evidenced by the fact that most people who reduce their weight through diet and exercise alone gain the weight back. Saying that diet and exercise are key to reducing your weight would be like saying the key to a college degree is reading a book. It is only part of the equation.

Speaking of college, we find a similar phenomenon among those who earn college degrees. Studies show an increasing number every year of people who graduate from college but fail to apply their degrees in the workforce. These individuals focus only on the *mind pillar.*

Likewise, I personally know several individuals who strive to become financially wealthy by focusing only on the *soul pillar*, which I divide into two subcategories: *emotional* and *spiritual*. These individuals believe the key to wealth is releasing negative emotion through energy work, meditating, and tuning their vibrational frequency to that of a wealthy person. While scientific data supports such activities, by themselves, they will rarely yield any financial gain. I do some form of meditation almost every day, but I've never had a bag of money fall from the sky into my lap while doing so. It is only when I focus on all three pillars that true change takes place.

Likewise, there are three steps to permanent change.

The first is *knowing*. Becoming successful is a process. It is important to learn all you can. If you dream of being a successful medical doctor, a major part of the process will be attending and graduating from medical school. If you dream of being a millionaire, a major part of the process will be learning how to create wealth the way millionaires do. Attend seminars, read books, listen to audio trainings, hire excellent mentors and coaches, and learn all you can about how to achieve all you desire.

The second step is *doing*. It doesn't matter how much you know until you actually *do* what you know. Learning how to be a millionaire doesn't help anyone unless you change your behavior and actually *do* what millionaires do. Likewise, you can read a lot of books about how to reduce your weight, but if you do nothing to implement what you learn, reading the books is a waste of time.

The third—and most important—step is *becoming*. There is a major difference between those who reduce their weight and those who *become* healthy, slim people; between those who win a million dollars and those who *become* millionaires. Most people who reduce their body weight gain the weight back because they simply go through the motions of diet and exercise. They reduce their caloric intake and increase their exercise for a period of time. Unfortunately, once they stop and go back to their old habits, they put the weight back on. Likewise, most people who win the lottery end up completely broke after a short time.

So how do you *become* the person you desire to become, thus achieving *permanent* results? It starts with creating a new *lifestyle* while focusing on all three pillars of growth.

Let's use the fitness category as an example. More than half of the American population is overweight or obese. Most people would prefer to be thinner, but they do nothing about it because they believe the process of reaching their ideal weight is one of deprivation, starvation, and torture. There is no enjoyment in cutting out all the foods you love. Some people do it for a period of time but eventually go back to their old habits (you can only torture yourself for so long). Thus the weight comes right back. In order to *become* a healthy and fit person, you have to focus on all three pillars. Diet and exercise are important components of the body pillar, but the mind and soul pillars are just as important. Unless you focus on the other two pillars, diet and exercise usually yield only temporary results.

Rachel enjoyed a slim body growing up. As a cheerleader, she was healthy, active, and loved her body. Early in her adult years, she became involved with a man who abused her in every sense of the word. After their breakup, she gained a significant amount of weight. At a subconscious level, she believed she would be more protected if she was heavier because fewer men who could potentially abuse her would notice her. Consciously, she hated her body. She tried several diet and exercise plans and always released five to ten pounds, only to gain the weight right back. Focused only on the body pillar, she achieved only temporary results.

It wasn't until a personal trainer who understood the three pillars of growth asked about her past that she realized her mental and emotional wounds needed to be resolved and healed for full transformation to take place. Once she focused on all three pillars of growth, she released eighty-five pounds in three months and one hundred forty pounds over the course of a year. She has kept it off and now enjoys life as a personal trainer. She didn't settle for simply a knowledge of how to reduce her weight. She didn't just go through the motions to achieve temporary success. She *transformed* and *became* a healthy, fit person.

Likewise, approximately half of all Americans live paycheck to paycheck. They are only one major financial setback away from bankruptcy. Most people would prefer to have more money, but they never do anything about it. Some read books written by millionaires, some attend seminars hosted by millionaires, and some listen to audio trainings created by millionaires; but they never change their behavior. They focus only on the mind pillar, never achieving more than a level of *knowing*. Some people invest in high-end mentoring to learn new skills and how to build a business, which they *do* for a period of time, focusing on the *body pillar*. Eventually, they give up and go back to their old way of life.

To achieve wealth, first *learn* the skills necessary to become financially wealthy and develop the mindset of a millionaire (mind pillar). Release any negative emotion and limiting beliefs surrounding money and success (soul pillar). *Do* whatever it takes (body pillar) to develop products or services that help people. Then market your products and services, build teams, make sales, and eventually automate the process. That's how you *become* a millionaire.

The same is true for all five F's of success. If you desire to increase your faith, study spiritual texts (mind), and go and do those things that bring you closer to the Divine, such as Sabbath Day worship and serving your fellow man (body). Turn your whole heart to the Divine while forsaking your imperfections (soul), thus *becoming* a more spiritual, saint-like person. If you desire to improve family relationships, study the words of relationship experts (mind); engage in appropriate physical touch, such as heart-to-heart hugs (body); and connect at deep emotional levels, while healing wounds from arguments and disagreements (soul). Thus you *become* a happy, joyful family.

Write the following in your success journal:

"To know < To Do < To Become. I transform into all I desire by focusing on all three pillars of growth: body, mind, and soul."

Now place your hand over your heart and declare, "I am amazing!"

Keep all three pillars in mind as you set goals. Ineffective goals focus on only one or two pillars at a time, such as, "I want to learn about human psychology (mind pillar)," or "I want to go running every day (body pillar)." Other ineffective goals are unmeasurable, such as "I want to earn more money." Simply saying you want "more" of something doesn't give your brain a clear target. When a person tells me he or she wants "more money," I hand that person a penny and say, "Goal completed. Now what?"

Some people make the mistake of simply focusing on a *feeling*, such as "I want to feel happier." As important as feelings are, in and of itself, this is ineffective because there is no way to measure a clear outcome. This is where many aspiring mentors and coaches get in trouble. They advertise their services as "helping people feel better about themselves" or "helping people gain clarity in their lives." As good as feeling better about oneself and gaining clarity are, these are not specific outcomes, which is what people pay top dollar to achieve.

Effective goals incorporate all three pillars of growth: a clear and measurable outcome (mind), a feeling that accompanies its achievement (soul), a clear purpose for the achievement (also mind), and clear action to ensure its achievement (body). An example, in the financial category of the five F's, might be:

I desire to have $10 million in the bank because I will feel peaceful, grateful and excited, which will allow me to spend an extra two hours per day writing my books to inspire millions of people to achieve their ideal lives in all five F's of success. To achieve this, I now 100 percent commit to spending thirty minutes per day reading books written by people who have achieved deca-millionaire status, sixty minutes each day making marketing phone calls to potential clients, and twenty minutes each day meditating and replacing any limiting beliefs with empowering beliefs, thus becoming a deca-millionaire.

Let's dissect that paragraph bit by bit.

I desire to have ten million dollars in the bank. This is a clear, measurable goal. You know exactly when it has been achieved.

I will feel peaceful, grateful and excited. These are the feelings the soul desires to have upon achieving the goal.

... which will allow me to spend an extra two hours per day writing my books to inspire millions of people to achieve their ideal lives in all five F's of success. This is the why, or the purpose, for achieving the goal. This is what your mind wants to know.

To achieve this, I now 100 percent commit to spending thirty minutes per day reading books written by people who have achieved deca-millionaire status, sixty minutes each day making marketing phone calls to potential clients, and twenty minutes each day meditating and replacing any limiting beliefs with empowering beliefs... These are the specific action steps (body) to take in order to achieve the goal.

... thus becoming a deca-millionaire. This is what you will *become* by achieving the goal.

Mind, body, and soul.

Knowing, doing, becoming.

Chapter 10: Three Pillars of Growth

In your success journal, follow this formula to set effective goals in all five F's of success:

I desire _____ (specific, measurable goal) because I will feel _____ (positive feelings), which will allow me to _____ (purpose for achieving the goal). To achieve this, I now 100 percent commit to _____ (daily action steps that incorporate body, mind, and soul), thus becoming a _____ (what you desire to become).

Again, do this for all five F's of success and put your five paragraphs on your wall next to your vision board to use as affirmations each day.

Now place your hand over your heart and declare, "I am amazing!"

Being Stuck Sucks, So Stop It!

CHAPTER 11
COMPLETING THE JOURNEY

Parable of the Tomato Plant

There once was a woman who dreamed of having a large, flourishing tomato garden. She saw the tomato gardens of some of her town's top tomato gardeners, and she decided it was what she wanted as well. She purchased a bag of tomato seeds at her local grocery store, and when she arrived home, stuck a single seed in the ground in her back yard, covered it with soil, and poured a cup of water over it.

"I can't believe it was that easy," she said to herself. "Pretty soon, I'll have a beautiful garden full of tomatoes!"

Several days passed, and she realized she hadn't been in her back yard since the day she planted the seed. She opened her back door and, to her horror, saw nothing but dirt in her yard.

"This can't be right," she thought. "I bought the right kind of seed. I thought all I had to do was plant it in the soil, and it would grow into a beautiful garden. What happened?"

She decided to investigate.

"Perhaps I have the wrong kind of soil," she thought to herself. "No, that can't be right. My soil is the same as my next door neighbors' soil, and they have a fantastic tomato garden.

"Perhaps it was because of bad weather? No, that can't be right, either. Again, my neighbors' tomatoes withstood the same weather.

"It must all be a scam," she finally decided. "The store that sold me these fraudulent seeds, the people in my neighborhood who 'claim' to have beautiful tomato gardens, which I bet are all fake anyway. I bet they're all in on it together just to make a quick buck from victims like me. Shame on all of them!"

She threw the remaining seeds into the garbage and vowed never to fall for such a hoax again.

What she failed to realize is the steps to growing and maintaining a beautiful tomato garden are:

1. Purchase seeds.
2. Plant many seeds.
3. Water and nourish the seeds until they sprout and grow fruit.
4. Repeat the process.

Many believe the process of creating an amazing life happens overnight. They learn about books that have changed many lives, seminars that have put people on the path to success, and the like. Believing all they need to do is read the book or attend the seminar, they purchase the book or the seminar ticket. But once they finish the book or return from the seminar, they complain that their lives haven't changed. These are the people who purchase seeds but never plant them.

Some read the book or attend the seminar, come home, and begin to apply what they've learned. But then they give up because their first attempt does not yield the fruit they hoped for. Perhaps they made a single prospecting call that did not yield any new clients. Perhaps they created a single online course that did not generate any revenue. These are the people who plant a single seed but give up when it doesn't sprout.

Others read the book or attend the seminar, then hire the author or presenter to mentor them to their desired outcome. Unfortunately,

Chapter 11: Completing the Journey

once they achieve their first goal, they disconnect from the mentor and slip back into old habits. Their life goes back to the way it was before they read the book or attended the seminar. These are the people who purchase seeds, plant many of them, and water and nourish the seeds until they sprout and grow fruit. Unfortunately, once they've picked the first batch of tomatoes, they stop caring for their garden, so the plants shrivel up, and the garden dies.

Finally, there are those who read the book or attend the seminar, hire the author or presenter to mentor them to their desired outcome, and continue to repeat the process. Their gardens flourish, grow, and expand. These people purchase seeds, plant many of them, water and nourish them until they grow and produce fruit, then repeat the process. They understand the importance of being *finishers.*

How many times have you started a project or set out to achieve a particular goal but stopped midway into the process? Failing to follow through and see goals to completion is a sure way of getting *stuck.*

Write the following in your success journal:

"I am a finisher. I finish every project I start. I see every goal through to completion."

Now place your hand over your heart and declare, "I am amazing!"

Ironically, *finishers* understand that many goals are never actually "finished."

"But, Eric, I had a goal to get my dream car, and I got it!"

Great. Now it's time to take great care of that car.

"But, Eric, I had a goal to release twenty pounds, and I achieved it!"

Great. Now it's time to keep the weight off.

"But, Eric, I had a goal to grow my business into a million-dollar company, and I did it!"

Great. Now it's time to grow it into a *multimillion*-dollar company.

Finishers follow a practice that Tony Robbins calls *CANI*, which stands for Constant and Never-Ending Improvement. Once one goal is achieved, they set a new one. Once one dream is reached, they find another. They understand that happiness comes from progress. They are grateful for all they have, enjoy the journey, learn from every failure, celebrate every victory, and never become complacent.

Remember the quote, "When you stop growing you start dying." This means there is no such thing as stagnation. Either you are moving forward, or you are moving backward.

This is another reason it is important to have both a vision board and a dream board. Each time you achieve a vision board goal, put another one on it. Repeat this process until you have achieved your dream board goals. Once your dream board goals have been accomplished, create a new dream board. It is an amazing process.

Write the following in your success journal:

"I practice Constant and Never-Ending Improvement. When I achieve a goal, I set another."

Now place your hand over your heart and declare, "I am amazing!"

"But, Eric, I am always busy, but I never seem to get any closer to achieving my goals. What gives?"

Many people get *stuck* because they confuse being *busy* with being *productive*. They fill their days with endless tasks that provide an illusion of productivity. In reality, their activities bring them no closer to achieving their goals than if they filled their days with blue screen time.

Write the following in your success journal:

"The number of hours I spend working matters much less than my levels of productivity."

What if you could accomplish twice as much in half as much time?

The following are eight tips that comprise what I call the *maximum productivity formula*. If fully implemented, the formula dramatically boosts your productivity, allowing you to get more done in less time.

1. **Always get a full night's sleep**. A common misconception among go-getters is that they have to train their bodies to survive on only a few hours of sleep in order to spend more hours working. Multiple studies have proved this simply doesn't work; those who consistently get six hours of sleep or less have the same cognitive performance as someone who is drunk. It's silly to attempt to get much done while drunk, but many go-getters do exactly that when they consistently get too little sleep. Make it a priority to get a full night's sleep. For some people, this means getting to bed by 9 p.m. and waking up at 5 a.m. every day. For others, this may mean going to bed at 2 a.m. and sleeping until 10 a.m.

    While some mentors swear that anyone who wants to be successful must be awake before dawn, I firmly believe the important thing is to find what works best for you. Some of the most successful people I know are night owls who get their best work done in the late hours of the night while everyone else is sleeping, then sleep in until late morning or early afternoon. As long as you put in the effort, consistently complete your inspired action steps, make progress, and see results, you don't need to worry too much about when you sleep; the important thing is getting enough sleep each night. The exceptions to this rule are those who thrive on *consistency* and need to *consistently* go to bed and wake up at the same time each day.

2. **No checking emails, text messages, voicemails, or social media for at least one hour after waking up**. This may take some getting used to because most people habitually reach for their phone first thing upon waking. The problem with this is whatever we put into our minds first thing in the morning sets up our whole day. One negative message can throw off your energy and productivity for the whole day if you read it within the first hour of

waking. The first hour after waking should be used exclusively for the following:
a. Prayer/meditation/connecting with the Divine
b. Gratitude work
c. Visualization
d. Listening to uplifting music, inspirational talks, books, or quotes
e. Stretching/yoga/exercise
f. Goal-setting
g. Positive self-talk

3. **Set certain times during the day when you *do* respond to your messages, and keep this commitment religiously**. Unless you are some sort of on-call emergency technician, turn off *all* notifications on your cell phone. Yes, *all* of them, including text messages, email, social media and phone calls. Keep your phone on *do not disturb* except during specific times you designate exclusively for responding to messages. I suggest setting aside one hour in the morning and one hour in the afternoon. Your employees and clients will get used to you not responding until those times of the day. They most likely aren't going to die if you don't get back to them immediately. Many people are controlled by the notifications on their phones. They check their messages far too frequently and respond to every notification they see. This drastically decreases productivity. Except for the time you designate to respond to messages, do not look at your phone the rest of the day unless you absolutely must. If two hours is insufficient you can make adjustments, but only after committing to the two hours until you break the habit of always checking your cell phone.

4. **Work for one hour at a time, and then take a ten-minute break**. Studies have shown that the most productive intervals of time for

work are from fifty to ninety minutes. Get tasks done for an hour without interruption (following tip three will greatly facilitate this), then take a break, go for a quick walk outdoors to reset your mind, and repeat the process.

5. **Focus on what is most important, not necessarily most urgent.** Life is full of distractions that mask themselves as urgencies. Make sure your inspired daily action steps take priority over simple "busywork." Actual emergencies are obvious exceptions, but things that appear "urgent" may be less important than other activities.

6. **Make proper nutrition a priority.** One of my favorite ways to alkalize my body (reduce acidity) and make sure I drink enough water is to consume green smoothies each day. This simple tool will help you have more energy, boost your metabolism, and increase your overall health. The healthier and more energetic you are, the more productive you will be.

    A few guidelines when making green smoothies:
    - It should not be fruit juice-based. Your base liquid for smoothies is filtered water. Fruit juice, especially from concentrate, is loaded with sugar and calories and can actually have the opposite effect of alkalization.
    - The main ingredient will be dark green, cruciferous vegetables, such as spinach and kale. They are the primary alkalizing component of the smoothie.

    The following is one of the most delicious and effective smoothie recipes you can find.

    (Recipe courtesy of SmoothieShred.com, Thomas Tadlock, M.S., author of *Miracle Metabolism*, shared with permission.)

Green Smoothie

Fill your blender three-fourths of the way full (packed) with organic spinach.

Add filtered water until it just covers the spinach.

Then add 1 ripe banana, 1 handful chia seeds, and 1 handful frozen pineapple.

Fill the rest of the blender to the top with frozen mango.

Blend on high for two minutes or until it reaches your desired texture.

Following this recipe will ensure you have a delicious, balanced smoothie that will help you stay hydrated, alkalize your body, and get your omega-3 fatty acids (from the chia seeds), which helps boost your metabolism. Drink one full smoothie every day.

Please note that, if you aren't used to drinking sixty-four or more ounces of liquid each day, this will likely make you go to the bathroom more frequently. I recommend finishing your smoothie at least four hours before going to bed so your bladder doesn't keep you awake at night. You will know you are on track to alkalizing your body when your stool becomes regularly green.

7. **Schedule one hour of personal "me time" (a.k.a. blue screen time) each day**. This time is used exclusively for doing whatever recharges you. This could be working on a hobby, reading a book, going for a walk, working out, or whatever helps you feel fulfilled and allows you to unwind.

8. **No electronics during the last hour before you go to bed.** The exceptions are if you use a meditation recording to fall asleep or

email yourself action steps to complete the next day. Avoid watching television, surfing the internet, or responding to messages right before you go to bed. Electronics reduce sleep quality, decreasing productivity levels. Instead, read a book, write in a journal, meditate, pray, and allow your mind to unwind from a full day of productivity.

Write the following in your success journal:
"I am highly productive. I follow the maximum productivity formula. I focus on completing what is most important rather than what seems most urgent. I drink a green smoothie each day for maximum energy."

Now place your hand over your heart and declare, "I am amazing!"

"Eric, this is amazing. If I'm a finisher, is there anything that could cause me to get *stuck?*"

Unfortunately, yes: *perfectionism.*

Perfectionism stops countless finishers in their tracks because they have the mindset that it isn't worth trying if they can't do it perfectly the first time. As funny as it may sound, perfectionism deters results because, no matter how hard you try, you will not be perfect in every way.

This is especially true when it comes to the body. The two main areas of the body people look down upon the most are the *belly* and the *bum.*

The key to overcoming perfectionism is to *love yourself more* and *forgive yourself faster.*

Right now, hold your hands out in front of you, then grab your belly. This seems silly, but do it anyway. Rub your belly for a moment. Maybe squish it a little bit. Then look at your belly and say, "I love you, belly. You're a good belly!"

Next, take your hands and grab your bum. Yes, actually grab your bum with your hands. (*your* bum, not the bum of the person next to you.) Say, "I love you, bum. You're a good bum!"

If you've never done this exercise before, you probably feel silly right now. But studies show that the more love a person sends to his or her body, the better that person's body functions. The more love you send yourself, even to the parts of your body you may not totally love, the more confidence you will have. The more confidence you have, the less power perfectionism will have over you.

Each morning, as you get ready in front of your mirror, give yourself a gentle rubdown and tell the parts of your body how much you love them. Yes, this will seem hokey at first, and that's okay. The more love you give yourself, the faster you will forgive yourself for being imperfect. You must allow yourself to be *imperfect* to become *perfect*. *Imperfection* is the only path to *perfection*.

Write the following in your success journal:

"I send love to my body every day. I quickly forgive my imperfections. By allowing myself to be imperfect, I progress toward perfection."

Now place your hand over your heart and declare, "I am amazing!"

Finishers receive the reward at the end of the journey, which is why I have a special reward for you for finishing this book. Each year, in Salt Lake City, Utah, I teach a transformational three-day seminar called "Lift Off" to help people just like you eradicate everything that has kept them *stuck,* thus transforming into the person they desire to be. As good as it is to *read* about these principles, it is much better to *experience* them. Tickets to this event are normally $1,750 each. Information, dates, testimonials, and a highlight video can be found at this website: https://www.feelwelllivewell.com/lift-off/.

Because you finished this book, your reward is a chance to attend this event with a guest at *no charge*. I must warn you: this event is only for those who are absolutely *serious* about never being *stuck* again. Only attend if you are totally committed to taking your life to the next level. To claim your free tickets, send an email

Chapter 11: Completing the Journey

to Office@FeelWellLiveWell.com with the subject line "Lift Off". Let my team know you have read this book and would like to attend the next seminar. Please include a phone number where you can be reached, and someone from my team will respond with dates and how to register with a scholarship code. I promise, if you attend and implement what you learn, your life will be much more fulfilling, and you will have the tools to ensure you never have to stay *stuck* again. You are worth it.

I can't wait to see you at the next class.

Congratulations for completing the training inside this book! Continue to implement what you have learned and share this book with those you feel would benefit from it. You are worth it. You can do it. You can live the life you deserve.

Now place your hand over your heart one last time and declare, "I am amazing!"

Acknowledgments

Special thanks go to the amazing mentors I have had in my life, including Heather Bailey, Kris Krohn, T. Harv Eker, Tony Robbins, Leslie Householder, Garrett Gunderson, Dr. Roland Phillips, and Dr. M. T. Morter Jr. Without you, your support, and all that you have taught me, none of this would have been possible.

About the Author

Eric Bailey is a professional mentor, trainer, and advanced holistic healthcare practitioner. Over the years, he has closely observed the habits of highly successful people. Implementing what he has learned, he has seen massive growth in his healthcare practice, health, and relationships, especially his relationship with his beautiful wife, Heather.

In one year alone, he grew his monthly income more than a hundredfold, going from welfare to wealthy. He now seeks to share his secrets to success, which absolutely anyone can use. Eric is a powerful motivational speaker and has impacted the lives of thousands of people through his audio training CDs, books, seminars, personal mentoring programs, and healthcare practice in northern Utah.

His greatest desire is to improve the lives of millions of people around the globe by helping them achieve vibrant health; massive wealth; and successful, loving relationships.

Being Stuck Sucks, So Stop It!

www.ingramcontent.com/pod-product-compliance
Lightning Source LLC
Chambersburg PA
CBHW070549010526
44118CB00012B/1267